THE
LINZ FILE

THE
LINZ FILE
Hitler's Plunder
of Europe's Art

Charles de Jaeger

Webb&Bower
EXETER, ENGLAND

Published in Great Britain 1981 by
Webb & Bower (Publishers) Limited
33 Southernhay East, Exeter, Devon EX1 1NS
In association with Limelight Limited

16 DEC 1981

Designed by Vic Giolitto

Copyright © Charles de Jaeger 1981

British Library Cataloguing in Publication Data
De Jaeger, Charles
   The Linz file.
   1. Art thefts – Europe
   2. World War, 1939–1945 – Destruction and
   pillage – Europe
   3. Hitler, Adolf
   I. Title
   707'.5   N9160

   ISBN 0-906671-30-2

Typeset in Great Britain by Keyspools (I.O.M.) Ltd./Man Photocomposition
Second Avenue, Onchan, Isle of Man.

Printed and bound in Great Britain by
A. Wheaton and Company Limited, Exeter.

CONTENTS

Preface

My interest in Adolf Hitler's grandiose plan to build a museum of European art at Linz, in Austria, began some time ago. In 1966 I produced, with Wynford Vaughan-Thomas, a film for British and American television, *Art in Peril*, which aroused considerable interest in the subject. The research for this documentary was very detailed, and during the course of a fact-finding tour round Europe I collected far more information than could possibly be crammed into a fifty-minute film: too many facts only confuse the viewer. The film itself concentrated on Hitler's career as an unsuccessful artist and the devastating effect he was to have on the world of art, once he rose to be dictator of the Third Reich. While working on the film I became interested in the question of whether Hitler the dictator could have been a product of Hitler the frustrated artist. Was the thwarting of his youthful dream to become a great painter or architect a contributory factor in starting him on the road to world domination? My researches indicated that Hitler's desire to gain absolute control of European art could be traced back to his boyhood in Linz, so I set out to interview people who could give me first-hand accounts of both his early artistic life and his later plundering of works of art. Since 1970, as official documents have been declassified, the full story of the Nazi art thefts has become much clearer. Many of the people I interviewed in 1965 have since died, but others are now more willing in their old age to talk about the past, though, understandably, many of them wish to remain anonymous.

I was in Europe throughout most of the period described in this book. In the 1930s I lived in Vienna, working as a journalist and then as a newsreel reporter, during which time I travelled regularly in Germany and Austria. I worked also for John Gunther in the preparation of material for his famous book, *Inside Europe*, published in 1936. As an on-the-spot newsman I was alert to the political and social situation. For events that took place in the war years I have relied on the documented reports of British and US Army fine arts officers.

In the pages following I have tried to piece together the story of Hitler's great dream of creating a world centre of German and European art in Linz; of Field-Marshal Göring's attempt, as a connoisseur of the arts, to amass a large collection of his own at his estate at Karinhall; and of the tug of war between these two men to gain possession of the masterpieces looted from the conquered countries of Europe. It is a story of intrigues, vandalism and profiteering which resulted in chaos, and in the destruction of vast numbers of irreplaceable treasures. Although many works of art were saved during the last days of the war, several thousand are still missing.

CHAPTER ONE

The Dreamer

In 1965, in the course of making a film, I walked up the Freinberg that overlooks the town of Linz, the provincial capital of Upper Austria. Standing there watching the lights of the town below, I remembered a story recounted by August Kubizek in his book *Young Hitler*. It was 1906, and Kubizek and Hitler had been to a performance at Linz's Stadtheater of Wagner's *Rienzi*, the story of a Roman dictator who ends his life, defeated and deserted by his people, in the ruins of his palace. It was a cold starlit November night and after the performance the two boys climbed the Freinberg together. Hitler had been deeply impressed by the opera; at the top of the hill he grasped his friend's hands and began to speak as if possessed. His plans for becoming an artist were temporarily forgotten; he spoke of a far greater future for himself, of tremendous powers that would one day be vested in him. Kubizek adds that in 1939, when Hitler was staying with Wagner's widow in Bayreuth, he told her that that night had been the turning-point in his ambitions.

Surrounded by wooded hills, Linz nestles in the Danube valley and since Roman times has been an important part of the shipping highway between Eastern and Western Europe. I had known this

9

small provincial town many years before the outbreak of World War II. Now in 1964 I had come back to start my investigations into Hitler's youth, his career as a failed artist, and its influence on his later plans to create the world's greatest art collection – purged of everything that displeased him – in the town where he grew up. Once Austria was annexed he started on his plan to make this quiet town a place of pilgrimage for art lovers. Here they would admire the greatest of art treasures in the finest museum ever built. The project was given Top Secret priority and known only to the inner circle of the Party hierarchy. The frustrated artist had by then truly acquired the power to realize his youthful day-dreams.

For my tracing of the story of the systematic destruction of 'degenerate' works of art, and the plundering of museums and private collections throughout Europe for the Top Secret project, Linz was the starting-point. I found that though the town had suffered badly from Allied bombing, it had been rebuilt in much the same style as it had enjoyed in pre-war days, and fortunately the old part of the town had suffered little damage. Many buildings must have been the same as they were when Adolf Hitler moved there with his family as a small child. Linz, then, was a small market town and seat of the provincial government. There was a large military garrison, and Linz 'society' consisted of the military, the civil servants, and a well-to-do business community. The town had a musical tradition of which it was justly proud. Anton Bruckner had composed symphonies while he was organist at the cathedral; the town orchestra gave frequent concerts under a talented conductor who had been a pupil of Liszt and worked with Wagner; there was an enterprising music society, the singer Richard Tauber was born there, as well as one of Austria's most celebrated writers, Hermann Bahr. In 1906 life in Linz was leisurely and pleasant, its citizens spending much of their spare time meeting friends or reading the newspapers in the coffee-houses. Nevertheless they worked hard too, and the young studied hard. Idleness was not acceptable.

This did not worry the young Adolf Hitler, strolling through the town immaculately dressed, sporting an ebony stick with an ivory handle and posing as a university student. Son of a respectable Austrian government official and his third wife, he had been born in 1889 in the frontier town of Braunau am Inn, poised between the territories of imperial Germany and of the Austro-Hungarian monarchy. When he was three the family moved across the border to Bavaria, where the child acquired the accent, characteristic of the region, that was to become noticeable when he grew older. Two years later they moved to Leonding near Linz. There the young Hitler was sent to the primary school run by Benedictine monks in the Abbey of Lambach, and he proved to be a good pupil. But when he moved on to secondary school his work deteriorated, he failed examinations, and was said to be lazy and temperamental. He did, however, show some ability in drawing. In 1906 he was being supported by his mother, his father having died in 1903, when they had moved to Linz.

The young Hitler was a misfit and a mother's boy. He had no time for coffee-house life, despised the sports that engaged his contemporaries, and had a particular hatred of civil servants (his father had wanted him to become one). Walking was his main activity. Later, as Führer, he insisted on roaming the streets at night, ostensibly unaccompanied, whenever he returned to Linz. An Austrian woman told me that when as a girl in 1938 she had been taking an early morning stroll along the Danube towpath with her dog, she saw, leaning over a railing, a lone figure in an overcoat and slouch hat. For a moment the man turned to look at her, and as she walked by she realized it was Hitler. He appeared to be without any bodyguard.

In 1906 Hitler was spending his time wandering by the Danube, up the Freinberg, mentally redesigning the buildings and sketching ambitious architectural plans. Up on the Freinberg he had a favourite bench overlooking the town where he would sketch and read. Evenings he often spent at the theatre, especially if a Wagner opera was being performed. He had no friends, or contact with former classmates, and it was at the opera that he struck up an acquaintance with August Kubizek. Kubizek was a music student and son of a local upholsterer, and in his book he describes how he got into conversation with a pale and skinny but well-dressed boy who was standing next to him in the gallery. They talked about music and found they had many tastes in common. Though they met again several times at the theatre and often walked home together after the performance, it was some weeks before Hitler told Kubizek his full name.

The two boys developed quite a close friendship. Hitler seems to have monopolized the conversations with his views on the arts, and Kubizek does not remember his expressing any political views. He showed Kubizek his sketches and watercolours, but Kubizek found them crude and uninteresting. Kubizek became very conscious – as many others were to do later – of Hitler's eyes and of his peculiarly penetrating gaze. He reports too that Hitler had frequent outbursts of temper and shouted excitedly in his Bavarian accent. His great ambition, Hitler revealed one day, was to become an architect or artist of genius.

I did not make much progress during my researches at Linz and it was not long before I came up against a complete blank wall. Later I discovered that I had approached the wrong people: the officials I contacted had had Nazi affiliations and, though they had since been 'de-Nazified' and kept their jobs, they had no wish to delve into the past and perhaps jeopardize their pensions by so doing. Nevertheless I managed to retrace the main steps of Hitler's early life there, and I took the opportunity of visiting his parents' grave in the cemetery nearby at Leonding. Mounted on the headstone were photographs of his mother and father. The grave was beautifully kept and had fresh flowers on it; somebody was evidently looking after it.

It was in 1906, at the invitation of relatives, that the young Hitler visited Vienna for the first time. Capital of the still mighty Austro-Hungarian Empire and under the rule of the elderly Franz Josef I, the city of imperial palaces, splendid uniforms and animated café life impressed the boy deeply. During Franz Josef's reign it had been transformed into a modern city. The Hofburg Palace and the summer palace at Schönbrunn were still supremely beautiful, but the old fortifications and walls which separated the centre of the city from its suburbs had been razed and a wide tree-lined boulevard, the Ringstrasse, built to replace them. On either side of it impressive new buildings were erected: law courts, museums, a new parliament in neoclassical style, a neo-Gothic town hall, and an opera-house modelled on the Paris Opéra. The magnates and nobles had vied with each other in employing famous architects to design their palaces. The outer suburbs had been improved by new housing which had replaced congested slums. From all over the Empire people of different races and languages converged on

Vienna in search of work and success. It was still the city of the waltz, of Lehar's *Merry Widow* and of Strauss and Lanner, both of whom gained fame and fortune there.

Hitler soon had to go back to Linz. But he had been dazzled by his first impressions of Vienna and was determined to return to the city. Meanwhile he resumed his old habits, wandering about the streets of Linz and day-dreaming. He would take a daily stroll down the Landstrasse, the town's main street; he regularly attended the theatre; and he came under the spell of Richard Wagner. And it was now that he replanned the whole town, with a new theatre, a new bridge over the Danube, and a great museum.

CHAPTER TWO

Disillusionment in Vienna

In September 1907 Hitler set off once again for the bright lights of Vienna, with his mother's blessing and financial support. He took some of his watercolours, for September was the month of the annual examinations for the Academy of Fine Arts and he still believed in his own artistic talents. He found accommodation with a Polish Jewish landlady off the Mariahilferstrasse, Vienna's main suburban shopping street. I found 29 Stumpergasse unchanged from the days when Hitler stayed there. A dingy one-storey house with a large courtyard and balcony running round it, its rooms were gloomy and the high apartment buildings nearly obscured the sunlight.

At the Academy of Fine Arts on the Schillerplatz, it was confirmed to me that, as his biographers have written, Hitler failed the Academy's examinations partly because of the lack of human figures in his paintings. There was a certain Professor Andersen, I was told, retired from his teaching post at the Academy, who might be able to help me further. A few days later I was able to meet the Professor – a charming gentleman then in his seventies. Had he known about Hitler's examination failure? Indeed he had. He had been taking the examination himself at the same time, and had sat next to the pale, thin youth. When the results were announced and Hitler found that he had failed, he flew into a rage. Andersen remembered how he stormed out of the room, muttering and cursing, and how afterwards he found him striding up and down outside the Academy. He buttonholed Andersen. Did he realize that the examiners were a lot of fossilized bureaucrats devoid of any understanding of young talent? The whole Academy ought to be blown up! It seemed useless to try to pacify him. In fact, out of 130 applicants only about thirty had been accepted. The standard was high and Hitler's work had simply not been good enough.

In *Mein Kampf* Hitler describes how astonished he had been when he heard he had failed the exam, for he had been so certain of success. Yet it is not hard to comprehend why he was rejected. Seventy-three years later I found myself looking at the three paintings he submitted for the examination, now hanging at Longleat House in Wiltshire, part of a private collection of sixty watercolours by Hitler, from his earliest days up to his Vienna and Munich period, collected by the Marquess of Bath. As can be seen from the paintings reproduced in this volume, they are quite agreeable to look at, pleasant enough scenes, but without much imagination.

Hitler lacked the determination to fulfil his own belief in himself. Many talented artists who had failed the routine Academy entrance requirements became successful with perseverance and further study. Hitler was in fact advised by the Rector of the Academy, Siegmund L'Allemand, to take up architectural design, but he would have needed school examinations to do that. It was a question of either working for school examinations again or of improving his painting with further lessons. He preferred to opt out, and returned to his Stumpergasse hideaway and a life of leisure.

At home in Linz his mother had been diagnosed as having inoperable cancer, and she was rapidly getting worse. Hitler returned home. Their kindly Jewish family doctor, Dr Bloch, could do nothing for her, and in December of that year, 1907, she died. Her death was a severe blow to Hitler and, since he had not yet reached his majority, a guardian was appointed for him. But he decided to go back to Vienna, to his former address.

In the spring of 1908 his friend Kubizek arrived to study at the Academy of Music. As he could not find anywhere to stay he moved in with Hitler, who persuaded the Polish landlady to give them a bigger room. Kubizek had no idea that Hitler had failed to get into the Academy of Fine Arts. Every day, he relates, his friend would go off to his 'studies' – in reality visiting the Hofburg Library, wandering about the city, sketching and dreaming his dreams of fame. It was only later that Kubizek learnt that Hitler had been rejected by the Academy. Perhaps Kubizek's own success was humiliating for his friend. As a music student Kubizek would get free concert tickets for the two of them. At the opera, however, they had to pay; it annoyed Hitler that army officers got in free, and he maintained that they went there only to see and be seen by Vienna society in the intervals. At that time the opera, under Gustav Mahler's direction, was full of vitality, producing great singers, and internationally famous. Enrico Caruso sang there in 1906 and 1907. In the theatres, new writers were flourishing and attracting large audiences.

In the world of art, the Secessionist group was at the height of its success and – in the decorative paintings of Gustav Klimt especially – was preparing the way for the *Art nouveau* style.* Klimt was an important forerunner of the genre and had contributed greatly to the decoration of many buildings and theatres of Vienna. In 1908 Oskar Kokoschka brought out his masterpiece in this style, a book called *The Boy Dreamers*. The Wiener Werkstätten, a joint organization of artists and craftsmen, was particularly influential in establishing the *Art nouveau* school, which found its supreme expression in sophisticated Vienna.

All this activity was flourishing around the young Hitler in the Vienna of 1908. But he knew little about it – and perhaps, obsessed by his grievances, did not want to know. In their shared room with its large piano he would lose his temper with Kubizek and pace the room like a caged animal. When Kubizek gave piano lessons to earn some pocket-money, he protested. His own taste in music was limited, though he had had piano lessons as a child. For him Wagner was supreme: *Lohengrin, Tannhäuser, Tristan and Isolde, The Ring*, he could listen to over and over again. Italian opera he disliked, apart from *Aida*. Of other composers he liked Bruckner and Beethoven, particularly the latter's Eighth Symphony.

As for his literary tastes, Kubizek records that he was an avid reader – of Nietzsche, Schopenhauer, Luther and Schiller – but that he never read in depth. Albert Speer has said that he seemed to read only the beginning and end of books. A particular favourite of Hitler's was Karl May, the German equivalent of

---

* The *Art nouveau* style was known in Germany as *Jugenstil,* and in Austria as *Sezessionsstil.*

Fenimore Cooper, whose tales of North American Indian life he matches in excitement. When Hitler became Führer he had a Karl May museum built for posterity, and he is reported to have told his generals – much to their embarrassment – that they should be tackling their campaigns in the Karl May spirit.

In 1908 the young Hitler was living in reasonable comfort. He still had money from his orphan's allowance and from what his mother had left him, and he had inherited a small legacy from an aunt. Meanwhile, he confided to Kubizek, he was working on a solution to Vienna's housing problems and had made some sketches, though on the whole he liked Vienna's new buildings and did not consider that many changes were needed. He continued to keep up the appearance of a young *Herr* or gentleman of leisure, but though he now spent some time in the coffee-houses his outlook was puritanical. He was impatient with the happy-go-lucky attitude of the Viennese, their way of living just for the day, and disliked the winebibbing in the 'Heurigen' inns.

There was one popular Viennese figure whom he did admire, and when he came to power himself he was to copy his ideas. Dr Karl Lueger, affectionately known by the Viennese as 'Der Schöne Karl' because of his good looks, was the powerful and much admired burgomaster or mayor of the city. Son of a house porter, he became a lawyer and then entered politics. He knew how to appeal to the lower-middle classes and especially to the 'little man' who regarded himself as an Austrian German and resented the influx of Czech, Hungarian, Polish and Slav nationals from the lands of the Austro-Hungarian Empire – and even more, the dominance of the Jewish intelligentsia in the arts, theatre, banking and other professions. Lueger was clever at exploiting anti-Semitism and all the other grievances. He was a good orator and knew how to mould a mass movement against capitalism as Marx had expounded it. His Christian Socialist Party had formed a coalition with the Pan-German Nationals and they made up a majority in the Reichsrat – the Parliament – against the already outdated Liberal Party. Lueger had four times won the majority vote for mayor of the city; but the appointment had to be ratified by the Emperor, and four times Franz Josef had refused to do so – partly on advice, but also because he was personally opposed to Lueger's anti-Semitism.

The Viennese resented the Emperor's attitude and staged their own silent protest. It was Franz Josef's custom, when he was living at Schönbrunn Palace, to ride down the Mariahilferstrasse in an open landau to Hofburg Palace. He was very popular among his people and they would greet him respectfully as he passed. But after he had turned down Lueger for the fourth time his friendly waving was politely ignored. The significance of this was not lost on him, and when Lueger was unanimously voted Mayor for the fifth time the Emperor did ratify the appointment. If he had done so earlier the Viennese might have benefited even more from some of Lueger's more progressive innovations.

Once installed in the town hall Lueger organized the public ownership of gas, electricity and the tramway system. By 1908 Vienna had the most modern power-station and the biggest tramway system in the world. All available open spaces in the city had been made into parks and public gardens, and a 'green belt' established round the city. Lueger built old people's homes and apartment blocks, and established savings banks. From the distant Raxalpe mountains he had a pipeline constructed to carry pure drinking water over viaducts into every Viennese home. He improved a health insurance scheme – Vienna was an important centre for medicine and surgery at the time. Lueger's premature death in 1910 was greatly mourned, and even the Emperor attended his funeral. To this day the Viennese owe a debt of gratitude to him as one of the founder modernizers of their city. Hitler, as he later admitted, was greatly influenced by him.

In the autumn of 1908 Hitler tried again, and failed again, to get into the Academy of Fine Arts. The same board of examiners were judging, and they found no improvement in the work he submitted. He returned dejected to his lodgings and then, while Kubizek was away in Linz, he moved out, disappearing from Kubizek's life without explanation. It seems that at this time he had begun to run short of money.

His next lodgings were in the Felberstrasse near the main Westbahnhof station. It was here that his growing anti-Semitism became reinforced. A few doors away from the lodging-house the violently anti-Semitic paper *Ostara* – named after the German goddess of spring – was on sale. Hitler became an avid reader of its theories about Nordic racial purity. *Ostara* was edited by a certain Hans von Liebenfels. Liebenfels's title was a sham. A former monk, he had left the order of the Holy Cross and become a more and more fanatical proponent of his racial dogmas. The centre of his movement was the ruined castle of Werfenstein. Here in 1909 he hoisted a flag with a red swastika on a gold background as the emblem of his racist party. Hitler actually went to see Liebenfels once, to get a back issue of the magazine. Liebenfels apparently felt so sorry for the shabby youth that he gave him the copy for nothing – but he had been impressed by him, he wrote to a friend.

There are conflicting reports of Hitler's movements in the winter of 1908–9. According to *Mein Kampf* it was a time of hardship – of painting, working as a labourer and sleeping rough. Some biographers, on the other hand, have maintained that Hitler cannot have been as poor as he made out, since he still had the orphan's allowance. Certainly he changed his address frequently and at one point joined forces with a down and out painter from Berlin called Reinhold Hanisch and moved into a men's hostel with him at 27 Meldemannstrasse. Though it has not been mentioned by his biographers, it seems he may in the meantime have been staying in a lodging-house in the Wurlitzergasse rather than living in the poverty he describes. In a Viennese expert's authenticated documentation of the Hitler watercolours in the Marquess of Bath's collection, the Wurlitzergasse address is given. Furthermore, the pictures had been sold to a picture-framer not far from there.

During this period in Vienna Hitler was certainly doing a great deal of painting and even selling his work to local shops. During my researches I visited an elderly Frau Hofrat K. who, I was told, might have one of his watercolours. Her apartment in the inner city was furnished with antiques and paintings, and by the window hung a small gilded frame containing a coloured drawing of an old Vienna scene with various people as well as horses and carriages, all rather crudely depicted. In the corner were the initials AH. In the summer of 1908, she told me, she had been strolling in the picturesque village of Grinzing below the Vienna Woods when she saw it in a picture-framer's window. The gilt frame was attractive and she decided it would do as a birthday present for her husband. The shopkeeper's price was reasonable. 'And how much for the watercolour?' she asked. She could have that for nothing, said the dealer. 'I only put it in to set off the frame. One of those young wandering artists gave it to me in exchange for a damaged frame he wanted. I picked it from his folder.'

I was most intrigued by its design: it was obviously copied from a print of the old Burgtheater before it was rebuilt in 1880. In the library that Hitler must frequently have visited (now the National Bibliothek) I found a history of the theatre, and in it a print that corresponded almost precisely to Hitler's picture. He had merely changed some of the figures.

Hitler's most productive period seems to have been during his stay at the men's hostel in the Meldemannstrasse. This was not a doss-house, as various biographers have stated. Built on the initiative of the Emperor and opened in 1906, it could accommodate 500 people and was considered a modern home for single men rather than an ordinary rooming-house. Retired officers and others with a small income stayed there. Each had his own cubicle with a bed, chair, table and space for clothes, and his linen changed once a week. There was a large reading-room and a lounge, washing facilities with showers, and a laundry-room. Cheap and substantial meals were available in the canteen, and for those who preferred to do their own cooking there was a separate kitchen. Hitler is thought to have prepared his vegetarian meals there. Hitler established his 'studio' in a corner of the lounge and there made detailed copies of postcards and drawings and coloured them in. His friend Hanisch would then hawk them round antique shops and try to sell them in restaurants in the nearby Prater pleasure-grounds. He sold regularly to a framer who liked to have a supply of cheap pictures to show off his frames. Hanisch claimed that Hitler was lazy and would turn out only enough work to keep himself in funds. The rest of the time he would hold forth on his ideas to anyone who cared to listen.

Hanisch had a fifty-fifty arrangement with Hitler, which was satisfactory to both sides, until one day Hitler accused Hanisch of keeping back some money from the sale of a watercolour of the Reichsrat building. Hitler reported this incident to the police, and Hanisch was kept in custody for a week. It has been suggested that he did not deny the charge because he was registered with the police under a false name. At any rate, that was the end of the business partnership. From then on it appears that Hitler sold directly to two Jewish dealers called Neumann and Morgenstern.

CHAPTER THREE

The Munich Artist

By 1913 Hitler had been in Vienna for five years. The monarchy was beginning to weaken, there were rumblings of revolution, and the Czechs and Hungarians wanted their independence. War-clouds were appearing on the horizon. Hitler had grown tired of his Vienna life. He disliked the Viennese, the Habsburg monarchy with its foreign nationals, and, last but not least, the Jews. Besides, his military service in the Austrian Army was already overdue and he did not want to serve. He packed his bags and entrained for Munich, the city filled with the atmosphere of Kaiser Wilhelm II's power and success. Here he could breathe freely, a German among Germans, and forget his Austrian setbacks. And the city was a great centre for artists.

He found himself a pleasant room in the artists' district of Schwabing, a few doors away from a house where Lenin had stayed. To play safe, he registered himself as stateless with the police. But he had reckoned without the long arm of Austrian officialdom. He was traced through the Austrian consulate and visited by the German police. After some correspondence about the short notice given him to report for duty in Vienna, the

Austrian authorities relented and allowed him to report to Salzburg. There – much to his delight – the verdict was that he was unfit for military service. It has been suggested that his failure to pass the medical examination was on account of his having flat feet, though this explanation is questionable in view of the fact that he was accepted into the German Army a year later.

On his return to Munich Hitler continued working as a copyist of postcards, producing careful watercolours of popular and saleable city scenes for an art gallery, such as the old town hall. These were popular as souvenirs for newly-weds, and he painted them so many times that in the end he could reproduce them from memory. But he remained an outsider in the artists' quarter. Kandinsky, Klee and Franz Marc were living and painting in Schwabing, and a new school of painting was evolving, but Hitler in his own little world was unaware of it. His artistic tastes had not changed. He favoured Karl Spitzweg, the self-taught Biedermeier painter who worked in Munich and immortalized the German small-town bourgeoisie.

For Hitler, World War I must have been a godsend, for although he was making a reasonably good living he had no real future as an artist. By now he was aware of this fact, and in later years he admitted that he had been only a minor artist who painted to earn his keep. He volunteered for military service and was accepted by a Bavarian regiment.

He proved to be a good soldier, attaining the rank of corporal, his non-military appearance, which did not inspire his comrades with much confidence, apparently being an obstacle to his gaining further promotion. Nevertheless he was twice decorated, with the Iron Cross first and second class, for bravery in the front line, and wounded twice. When he was off duty he continued to paint and, having no postcards to copy, he had to do so from nature. No doubt this explains why his surviving pictures of the time show a considerable improvement in design and colour on his previous work. These wartime pictures seem to have comprised his last efforts as a painter.

When the war ended Hitler immersed himself in politics. Having been demobilized he joined the National Socialist Party and soon became its leading figure. Judging by sketches produced in Munich in 1925 he was still interested in monumental architecture, however, and had not forgotten his youthful dreams of rebuilding Linz. Meanwhile, from 1923 onwards, Germany experienced one political upheaval after another – unemployment, gross inflation, and growing dissatisfaction among the middle classes – all of which Hitler was able to exploit for his own ends. In his youth he had seen how Lueger had climbed to power in Vienna, and he had always admired his intuitive grasp of popular feeling. The exponents of anti-Semitism and the doctrines of Aryan racial purity associated with the Pan-German ideal* – propounded by von Liebenfels, List and von Schönerer – were taken up by Hitler and their views developed. One result was his massive *Mein Kampf* (1924), later to become the bible of the Nazi Party and the biggest best-seller after the Bible itself. Income from the royalties was to make Hitler a rich man, the book being translated into many languages, and every Nazi home received a copy from the State. Today royalties from sales flow into the coffers of the government of Bavaria, which claimed ownership of all Hitler's possessions.

From 1925 onwards, while he was fully engaged in political work, Hitler supplemented his income in various ways – by writing articles for the Party newspaper, the *Völkischer Beobachter*, with foreign royalties from *Mein Kampf*, and also with money from the sale of photographs of himself. Helped by these extra resources he started a private collection of his favourite painters. One painter who had been a particular favourite of his since his youth was Hans Grützner, who specialized in nineteenth-century scenes of winebibbing monks and corpulent tavern-keepers. Hitler maintained that he would become the Rembrandt of the twentieth century and fetch similar prices. Thus he acquired thirty-one Grützner paintings. These ended up at the Meiserstrasse post-war clearing centre in Munich and proved to be of little interest to anybody, though today work by Grützner fetches a very high price on the German market.

What other painters did Hitler admire? His tastes, even to the end of his life, do not seem to have extended beyond about 1908. He liked all the early German painters: the brilliant naturalism and draughtsmanship of Dürer, Cranach's portraits and his reflection of the ideal German female beauty in the age of the

---

* The Pan-German or Gross Deutsche movement stood for a greater Germany incorporating all German-speaking territories within the then Austro-Hungarian Empire and under the rule of the German Kaiser.

Renaissance. He greatly approved of the work of the six-teenth/seventeenth-century Flemish master Brueghel and his wonderful evocation of rural merrymaking in the Low Countries. French eighteenth-century painters also attracted him. But in general it was the German and Austrian painters he held in most esteem, even the more obscure ones, with their meticulous draughtsmanship and colour. His taste was conditioned by his middle-class, provincial background. Of the Austrians, Rudolf von Alt was his favourite landscape artist and he had tried to imitate his style in his own work. Von Alt had studied at the Vienna Academy of Fine Arts, by which of course Hitler had been rejected. Hans Makart was another Austrian who had studied at the Academy. He had been dismissed for poor work and had con-tinued at the Munich Academy of Art under Piloty, but was eventually taken back by the Vienna Academy, which clearly recognized their earlier mistake, as one of their teaching professors. Hitler greatly admired Makart as a painter of the bourgeoisie and what they stood for. Then there was the land-scape artist Waldmüller, whose work was almost photographically accurate in style. He too had studied at the Vienna Academy and become a teacher there. Moritz von Schwind was another of Hitler's favourites.

Among the German artists, Hitler liked Anselm Feuerbach, an artist who attempted to revive the classical ideals of antiquity and embody his philosophy in them; but unlike the teachers of anti-quity he was able to reach only a tiny audience. He taught at the Academy and started to decorate the ceiling of the main hall with a series of compositions representing the war of the Titans, but he had to abandon the work because of ill-health, and it was left to others to complete it. Feuerbach had no great success in Vienna in expounding his philosophy through his art, and he complained bitterly of being misunderstood and of the neglect of his genius. He had wanted to become Germany's greatest monumental painter; but though he failed, he became widely known as a por-traitist. His autobiography, *Vermächtnis* (Testament), describes his early struggles in a somewhat self-pitying and pathetic strain. Hitler, during his reading sessions in the Hofburg Library in Vienna, must have read it and compared his own struggles with the author's.

I have picked out these artists because they had something in common: all had studied or taught at the Vienna Academy which rejected Hitler.

One painting that Hitler greatly admired is called *The Wild Huntsman*. It was painted by Franz von Stuck in 1889, the year of Hitler's birth, and still hangs in Munich's Lenbach Gallery. This work, based on the ancient Teutonic legend of a madman personifying death and destruction who rides forth at night leaving horror in his wake, shows a man running in a cloak and swinging a dagger, followed by a pack of wolves. He has black hair with a forelock, magnetic eyes, and a small brush moustache. It seems quite possible that on his Munich wanderings – he was always a great walker – Hitler became interested in von Stuck, to the extent that he decided to model his appearance, in a modified fashion, on the artist's terrifying image. His likeness to it is uncanny, and certainly Hitler emulated the legendary figure in his destructiveness. And there seems to be a further connection with wolves: not only did Hitler like to be called 'Wolf' by his intimates, but his favourite breed of dog was the Alsatian (wolfhound in German). When the Volkswagen factory was opened it was named after a nearby estate, Wolfsburg (wolf's lair). Hitler tried to persuade his sister, who looked after his home for a long time, to change her name to Frau Wolf. His secretary of twenty years' standing was a Fräulein Wolf. And according to one biographer, Walter Langer, Hitler liked to whistle the Walt Disney tune 'Who's afraid of the big bad wolf?' Moreover, all the various Führer headquarters near the front during World War II were named after this animal. Hitler's HQ in France was *Wolfsschlucht* (wolves' gulch), in the Ukraine *Werwolf* (were-wolf), and in East Prussia *Wolfsschanze* (wolf's lair). Often he referred to his SS men as his 'pack of wolves'. Again, it was the Werewolf youth units who were to spread death and destruction behind the Allied forces' advance into Germany – though that activity soon petered out. And towards the very end Hitler had with him in the Berlin bunker his favourite Alsatian dog. He had the animal put to sleep before shooting himself.

Throughout the 1920s Hitler drove a fast Mercedes and was popular in Munich society. Nevertheless he continued to yearn for acceptance by the artistic circles of Schwabing. One place he particularly liked to frequent was the Café Heck, a small establishment that seated about thirty people. As late as 1929 he would go there daily and sit at his *Stammtisch* (reserved table) with his Party followers – Strasser, Hess, Göring, and occasionally Goebbels. At another reserved table nearby a group of well-known Munich artists would meet. Among them was Richard Linder, a German Expressionist painter. Linder has told Dr Wolfgang Fischer, of Fischer Fine Art in London, about his almost daily encounters with Hitler at the café in 1929 when the Nazis were on their way to power. The group of artists would ignore the Nazis at the nearby table, or make derisive remarks in loud voices, but Hitler never rose to their taunts. He was always dressed in a black suit and black tie, says Linder, with a wide-brimmed artist's hat. Sometimes he wore black riding-boots, and he always carried a small dog-whip. At that time he made no great attempt to attract attention, and even appeared rather shy. He never raised his voice in conversation with his group, as Hess frequently did. He kept up the appearance of a respectable middle-class gentleman.

CHAPTER FOUR

The Art Supremo

Little did Lindner and his artist friends know what Hitler had in store for them when, only a few years before, they had seen him at the Café Heck. Hitler's purge of all the German art galleries was demonstrated in an exhibition in Munich in 1962 called 'Degenerate Art 25 Years Ago'. In 1965, from the exhibition catalogue and from other material I had accumulated, I realized that it was Germany's own museums and galleries which had suffered most, even before World War II started. Through research in archives and other sources I was able to piece together a picture of the 'degenerate art' campaign.

Although the philosopher of the Nazi Party, Alfred Rosenberg, had created a National Socialist Cultural League Society in 1928, contemporary artistic circles took little notice of it at the time. The Society promoted the idea of pure Nordic German art, in contrast to what they termed 'Bolshevik' ideals; an idea to appeal to the discontented 'little man'. Then with the first Nazi Party electoral breakthrough in 1930 in the Thuringia *Landtag* (Provincial Diet), an ex-policeman from Munich, Dr Frick, became the local minister for education.

Frick was a leading Nazi and the first to start the assault on modern art. His first target was the Weimar Castle Museum with its extensive collection of valuable paintings. The curator was dismissed, and the Nazi-appointed one who replaced him lost no time in putting the new policies into effect. Frick's art adviser immediately had the modern wall frescoes of Oskar Schlemmer whitewashed. Under the guidance of Hans Severus Ziegler, Reichspresident of the Chamber of Visual Arts who was later to become Hitler's art exhibition adviser, a commission arranged for all so-called 'degenerate' art to be removed from the collection. Over seventy paintings by modern artists were taken, including pictures by Klee, Kandinsky, Kokoschka, Otto Dix, and Nolde. Minister Frick declared that these paintings had no connection with the Nordic German character and represented a racially inferior humanity.

Worse was to come, and there was a precedent for what was to follow. The cleansing of Germany's museums of what Hitler in 1933 called 'Jewish-inspired Bolshevik art' was not the first of such operations. With his Party well established and by 1930 holding 107 seats in the Reichstag, Hitler in 1933 became Chancellor with greatly extended powers. A new ministry for 'enlightenment and propaganda' (Volksaufklärung) was created, with Goebbels at its head. The new policies towards art were becoming all too clear. Hitler denounced the internationalization of the arts; their renewal could take place only on German soil, he declared. Thus one German museum after another had its modern art collection confiscated. The curator of the Karlsruhe Museum was dismissed and replaced by an unknown Nazi painter, who organized an exhibition called 'Government Art between 1918 and 1933' which maligned Impressionist and Expressionist art as degenerate. Mannheim Museum came next. There valuable modern paintings were taken out of their frames and rehung in a haphazard fashion. All the German museums and galleries were stripped of non-Nazi modern art by Hitler; in fact the German museums' losses were greater than those suffered by any other country.

When the first purges of modern art were carried out the German press criticized them. In a new magazine, entitled *Kunst am Volk* (Art of the Nation), an attempt was made to achieve a discretionary balance between the new Nazi policies and the trends of modern art, and even to defend Expressionism. But

Hitler would tolerate no criticism, eventually prohibiting it altogether, and after two years the magazine was officially closed down for being anti-Party in outlook.

Distinguished German artists protested to Goebbels about such activities as these but were ignored. Some even expressed their disgust in their paintings: Beckmann, in the second decade of the century, was already creating a vision of the terror that was to come; Kokoschka expressed his revulsion in political drawings. In previous centuries various artists – Hogarth, Goya and Daumier, for example – had employed similar methods of protest. Goebbels himself, as president of the Reich Chamber of Culture, had realized the dangerous trend of this art censorship earlier and had made a speech guaranteeing the freedom of the arts. Even in a National Socialist state, art could survive only if it were left to develop unhindered, he maintained. But Hitler was not deflected, and his determination to stick to his policy affected even his own ministers.

One of Hitler's aims in his new role as Chancellor of the Reich was to make Munich, birthplace of the Nazi movement and his second home after Linz, into a great centre of German art. According to some sources, he had already drawn up plans for a national museum there by 1925. In 1933 he instructed Professor Paul Ludwig Troost, his chief architect, to set about designing the new Haus der Deutschen Kunst (House of German Art). It was to replace Munich's celebrated Glaspalast Gallery, which had been destroyed by fire in 1931 with the loss of over 3,000 valuable German paintings, and it was to contain only nineteenth- and twentieth-century German works, arranged to Hitler's own plan. On the day the foundation-stone was laid Hitler declared in an emotive speech that this was to be the new centre of German art, a temple dedicated to the goddess of art. A small incident, unnoticed except by those standing close to him, somewhat marred this much-heralded opening ceremony. To their embarrassment, the delicate handle of the specially designed hammer snapped off when Hitler tried to tap the stone into place. It seemed a bad omen, and those who saw it knew how superstitious Hitler was. The bandmaster, however, noticed what had happened and saved the day by striking up some rousing music.

Throughout the 1930s the Nazi tornado swept through the world of German art, slowly at first but with increasing force. The crunch came in 1937 when the Berlin National Gallery was forced to close its exhibition of modern art and its director, Dr Eberhard Hanfstaengl, resigned in protest. An official document was released by the Reichskammer for Cultural Affairs giving new instructions to be followed by all museums and galleries and by artists. All the arts were affected – music, literature, theatre and cinema as well as the visual arts.

The confiscations, no longer reported in the German press, continued. Adolf Ziegler was now appointed by Hitler as adjudicator of all paintings and sculptures, empowered to take into State ownership 'for safe keeping' – the new term for confiscation – all 'degenerate' art produced since 1910. The illegality of this edict was of course ignored by Hitler. The newly appointed 'Professor' Ziegler – Hitler personally created titles for those of his favourites who did not have the right qualifications – set up a commission with three other members. Among them was a Count Baudissin, the newly installed Nazi curator of the Volkswang Museum at Essen. His first self-appointed task was to clear his own museum of 'degenerate' art: over 1,200 pictures from the most valuable modern collection in Germany were confiscated. The commission removed 900 modern paintings from the Hamburg Kunsthalle and over 1,100 from Berlin galleries. A detailed account of the events affecting the gallery, published in the Prussian museum authorities' yearbook in 1970, reveals the full extent of its losses.

Berlin galleries quickly returned any modern pictures on loan to their owners, and the National Gallery spirited away many pictures – by Picasso, Braque, Munch, Feininger, Dufy and others – that had been donated by the gallery's Society of Friends, and deposited them in the vaults of the Thyssen Bank, where they remained. Museum curators throughout Germany were warned in advance of an impending visit by the Ziegler commission. The commission would arrive with a detailed list prepared in advance of all the 'degenerate' art housed in a museum, and anything that was considered at all modern was condemned.

After the commission's initial visits – more were to follow – the Berlin National Gallery lost 164 paintings, twenty-seven modern sculptures and 326 drawings and watercolours. Many of these were earmarked for the great exhibition of 'degenerate art' that was being planned. Then the curator of the modern art department took action. He removed the most important items from this first heap of confiscations and replaced them with similar but less valuable works of art, the main thing being that the right number were taken away. Many important pictures by Munch, Kirchner, Picasso and others were saved in this way. Other pictures were stored away out of sight, among them Kokoschka's *Portrait of Adolf Loos* (1909) and Kirchner's *The Rhine Bridge at Cologne*.

Göring, as head of the Prussian State, did not approve of the commission's activities, but he could not countermand an order coming direct from Hitler. The art policy had compensations for him, however. He had decided that he needed more tapestries for his estate at Karinhall, and he arranged a system of exchange by which 'degenerate' works of art were exported in exchange for valuable Gobelin tapestries available on the art markets of Europe. His excuse was that one day, after his death, Karinhall would belong to the nation. Most of the pictures exchanged had been confiscated from the Berlin National Gallery, among them some paintings by Munch and three by Van Gogh. Some were sold to Norway by the art dealer Haberstock, on Hitler's instructions. When a painting was sold abroad, the museum from which it had been taken was partly reimbursed in Reichsmarks. Franz Marc's large painting, *The Tower of the Blue Horses*, which was sold abroad on Göring's behalf, is still missing. It was destined for the forthcoming show of 'degenerate' art in Munich, but was removed as a result of protests by the League of German Army Officers. Marc had been an officer in the Imperial German Army in World War I and was killed at Verdun in 1916.

According to official Nazi records, about 16,500 valuable paintings, drawings, and sculptures, all classified as degenerate, were taken from just over a hundred museums all over Germany.* They were transported to a central collecting-point and sorted out according to their value. The Ziegler commission selected the ones destined for the exhibition of 'degenerate' art that was to be held in Munich to coincide with the opening of the new Haus der Deutschen Kunst – the Nazi temple of the new German art.

The inauguration ceremonies for this impressive building designed by Troost (who meanwhile had died) opened with a great parade through the beflagged streets of Munich. There were floats

* This total included 378 works by Lyonel Feininger, 295 by Lovis Corinth, 509 by Max Beckmann, 417 by Oskar Kokoschka, 639 by Ludwig Kirchner, 1,052 by Emil Nolde, 688 by Karl Schmidt-Rotluff, as well as work by Paul Klee, among many others.

depicting Teutonic legends and episodes from German history. Dressed as Teutonic warriors, perspiring men manhandled ash trees of tin foil – according to Nordic myth the ash joined Heaven, Earth and Hell. Columns of women followed, dressed in the costumes of Dürer's and Cranach's times. Altogether there were over 3,000 people parading in costume, followed by another 3,000 marching in the modern part of the parade, which ended with Nazi military formations. The new building had an impressive exterior, with a portico extending almost the entire length of the front. Troost had designed it on the basis of Hitler's own sketches and it embodied Hitler's conception of the ideal German monumental architecture. But Hitler had copied from the past again. After the defeat of Napoleon, Kaiser Wilhelm I had instructed the classical architect Friedrich Schinkel to build a gallery in which his own private collections could be shown to the public. It formed the nucleus of the Old Berlin Museum, and it too had an imposing façade with a portico. The difference was that the Kaiser had exhibited Europe's finest works of art, while Hitler's officially approved exhibits merited the jibe that they were housed in Munich's new Art Terminal.

On the opening day of his new museum Hitler made a typically verbose speech praising the new Nazi era in art and its great future. The 900 exhibits on show and the first great display of paintings and sculptures had been personally approved by Hitler himself. He was the final judge – and was to continue to be so for all the annual exhibitions at the Haus der Deutschen Kunst in future. Hitler's opening speech was reported at the time in the monthly *Kunst im Dritten Reich*. Reading it now, it seems scarcely believable that such a rant could have been accepted: '. . . Dabblers in art, modern one day and forgotten the next; Cubism, Dadaism, Futurism, Impressionism, Expressionism; all utterly valueless to the German people. . . . Nobodies without any talent; dilettantes who should take their scribbles back to the caves of their ancestors. . . .' He intended, proclaimed Hitler, to take drastic action against these last elements of subversion. It seems very much as though he were out to wreak personal revenge on the artists who were successful in the period before World War I, when he failed so totally at his own painting. In this context there is an interesting sidelight. In a circular letter issued by Goebbels, marked 'Confidential' and sent out to the various

Adolf Hitler aged sixteen. Sketch by a
fellow-pupil at school.

Linz, Austria. The main square at
about the time Hitler was born in
Braunau am Inn. Beyond the square is
the old stone bridge across the Danube.

(*Left, above*) A Vienna coffee-house in 1907.

(*Left, below*) Emperor Franz Josef I seen alongside Mayor Lueger during the laying of a foundation-stone in Vienna in 1906.

(*Right*) Cover of the magazine *Ostara*, which Hitler read in Vienna and which developed his anti-Semitism. This edition, of April 1906, proclaims : 'Revolution or evolution ? A free conservative Easter sermon for the masters of the European race.'

(*Below*) The Academy of Fine Arts in Vienna at the time Hitler failed his entrance examination.

Vienna Opera Square before World War I

Inner courtyard of Imperial Palace
in Vienna before World War I

The Vienna Houses of Parliament (Reichsrat)
The Wild Huntsman by Franz von Stuck, a painting greatly admired by
Hitler. It seems prophetic in its likeness to Hitler himself, and in fact Hitler
may well have modelled his appearance on the legendary Teutonic figure.

Hitler's sketches for a villa that he proposed building for his friend August Kubizek
Sketch by the eighteen-year-old Hitler for a concert hall at Linz

Hofbrauhaus, Munich by Adolf Hitler
Suburban House in Old Vienna by Adolf Hitler

Karlskirche, Vienna by Adolf Hitler

The Houses of Parliament, Vienna
by Adolf Hitler

provincial artistic directors at the time of the exhibitions of 'degenerate' art and of Nazi art, it was stated that at the Führer's request no exhibitions of his own work were to be staged.

A Swiss paper had commented on this exhibition that white plaster sculptures offended Hitler's taste, and he ordered them all to be coated with bronze paint. The art-loving Munich people have their own brand of humour, and they called the new museum with its 900 mediocre exhibits the Weisswurst Palast (White Sausage Palace), after Munich's famous white veal sausages. Other names were the palace Kitschi (Trash Palace) and the Palace of Pure Corn. There was no rush of visitors to view the pictures of peasant life, the grim portraits, and the representations of ideal Third Reich types. Much to the Nazi's chagrin the 'degenerate' art at the nearby Hofgarten was attracting over 20,000 visitors a day. Over 2 million people went to it in Munich alone. This was not at all what the Nazis had wanted.

The Haus der Deutschen Kunst exhibition was to become an annual affair, with Hitler always selecting the exhibits. He depended a good deal on the professional advice of Frau Troost, widow of the architect, and on that of 'Professor' Ziegler and of his court photographer, 'Professor' Heinrich Hoffmann. Ziegler, well known for his photographically exact paintings of female nudes, was widely known as 'Reichskommissar of the Pubic Hair'.

The author Reinhard Müller Mehlis has related an amusing story about the selection of pictures for the exhibition. The well-known Nazi painter Paul Mathias Padua had for a long time planned a picture of Leda and the swan. Leda was the wife of the King of Sparta, loved by Zeus in the form of a swan. Padua took a year to find the right red-haired model for Leda and had a swan specially killed and stuffed for this purpose. The resulting painting was very suggestive. When they saw it at the Haus der Deutschen Kunst before the exhibition opened, both Frau Troost and Professor Hoffmann were uneasy. The Munich state commissioner for museums, Gauleiter Wagner, was equally doubtful. The picture might corrupt the young – what were they to do? They decided to take the bull by the horns and speak to the Führer. The three of them went to the nearby Osteria Bavaria, the popular artists' restaurant where Hitler liked to take his meals. They explained their worry about the picture to him and Wagner pointed out that it was unsuitable for the young. Hitler decided to take a look at the offending erotic painting there and then. On seeing it he proclaimed at once that he liked it and that it must certainly be hung. When Wagner expressed his doubts again Hitler told him to shut up and strode out of the building.

For Padua, the artist, this incident had unfortunate consequences. Wagner was so furious at being snubbed by Hitler in front of the others that later on he accused Padua of writing a letter criticizing Nazi policies. As a result Padua was banned from Munich and had to retire to his country house on the Tegernsee. There he produced a painting of a German family listening intently to the Führer's voice issuing from the radio: this had been commissioned by the State Radio as a novel piece of propaganda. The picture of Leda and the swan, meanwhile, became very sought after, and was snapped up by Martin Bormann, Hitler's private secretary.

Göring, who did have taste and knew what he was buying, also pilfered from the 'degenerate' art that had been confiscated, and picked out some of the best items on the quiet for his private collection at Karinhall. He evolved a successful system for acquiring valuable works of art for nothing. On the occasion of his birthday or of annual festivities, wealthy industrialists would present him with a painting, having found out in advance from Göring's art dealer what the Reichsmarschall was looking for. And I was told by a museum curator in Vienna that there was consternation if Göring made a point of admiring a painting during a visit to a museum – it was usually a hint for the museum authorities to present it to him. Therefore pictures would sometimes be temporarily removed in advance of his arrival. Already by 1936 he had ordered the curator of the Kaiser Friedrich Museum in Berlin to send Rubens's *Diana at the Stag Hunt* to his Leipzigerstrasse residence. For their part the Vienna Kunsthistorisches Museum authorities were unlucky enough to be asked to lend some tapestries to the Reichsmarschall, a request which, after the Anschluss in 1938, they could not refuse. The whereabouts of the tapestries remain unknown.

As time went on it became a habit among the Nazi leaders to have so-called 'loaned paintings' in their offices and even their homes, and in Ribbentrop's case in his foreign embassies. There was a perpetual tug of war, it seems, between reluctant museum authorities and Party leaders. It became a matter of prestige, not only for the top echelons of the Party but for the smaller fry, to surround themselves with what were considered, in deference to the Führer's liking for German Romanticism, very valuable paintings. Much to Hitler's annoyance, fakes were produced of his favourite Spitzweg, and he could not be sure if the ones in his own collection were genuine or not.

Hitler continued to wage war on the modernists as he had promised in 1937 in his opening speech at the Haus der Deutschen Kunst. Unless an artist had applied to join the union founded by Goebbels and had been accepted, he was ostracized. Many decided to leave Germany. Lyonel Feininger returned to his homeland, the United States, Paul Klee to his native Switzerland, while Kirchner was already living in Davos. The confiscation of a lifetime's work affected Kirchner so much that he committed suicide. Secret instructions were issued by Goebbels to the German press in 1937 that none of the modern painters were to be mentioned in reviews – Barlach, Marc, Kokoschka, Nolde. The Reichskammer even demanded that Nolde hand over two years' work. In his book *Inside the Third Reich* Albert Speer recalls an incident, concerning Nolde's work, from the time when as a young architect he was engaged to redecorate Goebbels's new Berlin residence. Speer knew that Goebbels had better taste than Hitler and liked modern art. To embellish Goebbels's sitting-room he borrowed some watercolours by Nolde from the Berlin National Gallery. Goebbels and his wife were delighted with the effect, but when Hitler visited them and saw the pictures he ordered Goebbels to have them removed at once – despite that Nolde was accepted by the Nazis and was even a Party member.

Göring, meanwhile, issued his own new directives suppressing 'degenerate' art in Prussia. And those who failed to pay the so-called 'refugee tax' had all their property confiscated – a move against rich Jews and opponents of Nazism. Art publications which did not conform to the new policies were banned; foreign art magazines were not allowed into Germany; no one was to be allowed to read about modern art in other countries. Foreign currency was in short supply, the export of the Reichsmark was limited, and travel abroad became more difficult for everyone. In London, in 1938, a Nazi lecturer was declaring that there were signs of degeneracy even among the Old Masters. The Nazis rejected Rembrandt, 'the painter from the ghetto', said a Herr

Hansen in a talk he gave to museum directors under the auspices of the German Ministry of Education.

At the Berlin Art Gallery, while it was closed, two attendants managed to hide a picture by Erich Heckel, *Madonna of Ostende*, and to telephone the artist in secret telling him to hide his other pictures because there was going to be a raid. Heckel's paintings were classified by the Nazis as representing the very depths of decadence, and over 700 of his paintings were confiscated, the second largest number after Nolde's. He was forced to go underground, as were other artists. Carl Hofer, for example, was already being attacked in the Nazi paper *Angriff* for his work at the Berlin Academy of Art. How much longer was the Jew Hofer going to be in charge, it demanded? Ironically, Hofer was in fact of unmixed Aryan descent. He was, he himself declared, of all the artists, the one most hated by the Nazis, and the first to be dismissed from his job. He was prohibited from working and from exhibiting or selling his paintings, and was under constant Gestapo surveillance. Many of his pictures, consequently, were never sold, though some were selected for sale at the Lucerne auction described later in this chapter. In 1943 his flat and studio were wrecked, 150 paintings and over a thousand drawings being wantonly destroyed.

The 'degenerate' art exhibition, with its captions denigrating both the artists and their paintings, went on tour in Germany after its opening in Munich, and on the annexation of Austria it was shown there too. The pictures had been taken out of their frames and were hung at random in order to give an impression of chaos. 'How a Jewish artist distorts a rural German scene' was a typical Nazi caption. The aim was to demonstrate that Jewish and Bolshevik artists were responsible for a horrific decline in the arts since the beginning of the century. Many of the artists, however, were not even Jewish. Since the Austrian galleries contained few modern works of the type the Nazis considered degenerate, they did not suffer the same fate as the German ones. The exhibition did go on show in Vienna.

After the 'degenerate' art had toured Germany and Austria, a new decree on the 'safeguarding' of these paintings became law, laying down that no German museum would be compensated for its losses. The confiscations, in short, had become legal. Unfortunately after World War II the decree was not rescinded by the Allied occupation authorities, and anyone who had bought one of the confiscated works of art remained its legal owner. At the height of the confiscations, however, a couple living in Italy decided to try to salvage something from Nazi hooliganism.

Emanuel Fohn was an Austrian painter and his wife was from Munich. They approached the authorities in Berlin and proposed an exchange: Fohn would swap 200 items from his valuable collection of Romantic drawings and paintings for an equal number selected by him from the confiscated modern paintings. The Nazi authorities considered the offer mad but had no intention of passing it up, and the exchange took place. During the Allied bombing of Innsbruck the Fohns' house was hit and caught fire, but they were able to save the pictures. After the town had been liberated by the Allied forces they received offers for their collection from Swiss dealers. The money would have provided food and comforts for them, but they refused to sell. In spite of having sacrificed their own valuable collection, the Fohns regarded themselves as the guardians of the pictures and not the owners. At the age of eighty-four Herr Fohn presented the entire collection – including Kokoschkas, Klees and Kandinskys – to the Bavarian State Gallery. They are there to this day.

When eventually the 'degenerate' art exhibition came to an end the paintings were returned to the depot in the Köpenickerstrasse in Berlin, and the question then arose of how to dispose of them. An official in the Ministry of Propaganda outlined a solution to Goebbels. Let the valuable paintings be sifted from the inferior ones and offered to art dealers from abroad. Their disposal would bring in much-needed foreign currency. The unsaleable ones, in a symbolic gesture, should be burned (the disused granary in which they were stored was needed again). Goebbels agreed to this plan, and in March 1939, in the courtyard of the main Berlin fire station, 1,004 oil-paintings and 3,825 drawings and graphic designs went up in smoke.

The Berlin art dealer Haberstock, who was also the main buyer for Hitler's private collection, arranged for an auction of the remainder of the confiscated paintings through his Swiss contacts, a leading art gallery in Lucerne. It was held in June 1939 in the Grand Hotel National. Though many international dealers boycotted it, many others, as well as collectors, museum curators and art critics, turned up for this much-publicized affair. One hundred and twenty-five modern works of art confiscated from German museums were up for sale. The bidding did not go as expected. The *Daily Telegraph*, reporting on the sale in July, revealed low prices: Van Gogh's famous self-portrait from the Munich State Gallery fetched only £8,330; a Gauguin from the Frankfurt State Gallery £2,380; while Picasso's *Two Harlequins* was sold to an Antwerp museum for £3,800. Swiss galleries acquired some of the pictures, various foreign buyers saving others. The Van Gogh self-portrait went to the United States, Gauguin's *Tahiti*, from the Frankfurt Museum, to Belgium, along with a Picasso. Marc's *The Red Horses*, from Essen, stayed in Switzerland. A painting of Tower Bridge by Kokoschka, from Hamburg, went to America. In all, just over 570,000 Swiss francs were netted. Most of the German Expressionist pictures remained unsold, and shortly after the outbreak of war the Lucerne gallery sold them off to a Swiss dealer for the paltry sum of 4,000 Swiss francs.

CHAPTER FIVE

The Hero's Return

On 13th March, 1938 the death-knell had sounded for Austrian independence. The frustrated artist and dreamer who, twenty years earlier, had been ignored by the citizens of Linz, was returning in triumph. Crossing the River Inn at Braunau, his birthplace and the frontier between Germany and Austria, Adolf Hitler received a tumultuous welcome. Nazi flags hung from every house, the towns were decorated with flowers – even the cows had their flanks daubed with swastikas. His entry into Linz itself produced an even more overwhelmingly enthusiastic welcome for the town's long-lost son, especially from the young. Nazi subversion had by now successfully undermined Austrian ideals. During my various stays in Austria I had witnessed for myself how Nazi ideology had taken over, even among my own former school friends and close acquaintances. Even some of the foreign press correspondents were biased in favour of a Nazi take-over. While today one might have reservations about the enthusiasm proclaimed in some of the press reports, doubt cannot be cast upon the evidence of the newsreels showing Hitler's triumphal progress into annexed Austria.

The following day Hitler and his motor cavalcade proceeded through towns and villages hung with flags to Vienna. Everywhere he received an enthusiastic welcome, which reached its peak as he drove slowly down the Ringstrasse to the town hall. While the celebrations continued and Hitler was installed in the

Hotel Imperial, the chanting crowds outside repeatedly made him come out on to the balcony to acknowledge their enthusiasm. Meanwhile, behind the scenes, more sinister activities were quietly taking place. Himmler with his SS troops and the Gestapo had quickly and silently moved in on the city. All opponents of Nazism were rounded up and arrested. Jewish homes were broken into, and former friends now turned out to have been illegal Austrian Nazis and appeared in the uniforms of Storm-troopers or the elite SS. Without any assistance from their German colleagues they took the law into their own hands and helped themselves to what they regarded as their rightful loot. Later many were arrested by their German Nazi colleagues, tried and imprisoned – some even being sent to Dachau. As for confiscations, the Austrian Nazis discovered to their disgust that they could not get clean away with their loot. All possessions – bank accounts, safe certificates, shareholdings, etc. – had to be registered with the Gauleitung (regional leadership).

The brutality of Austrian members of the Party, in or out of uniform, has been well documented in the fictionalized experiences of Madeleine Duke – *The Bormann Receipts*. The father of Mrs Duke was a high official in the Austrian Government and she herself was present when the family's valuable collection of paintings was looted. The existence of the collection had been betrayed by a picture restorer who had worked on the paintings. The recipient of the collection was Martin Bormann. Some of these paintings have been traced and returned, while those that are still missing are believed by the owner to be tucked away in some official depot in Germany.

A day after his entry into Austria Hitler made a speech to a massive audience from the balcony of the Neue Hofburg (Imperial Palace) on the Heldenplatz. It was a well-organized affair. Austria was now part of the German Reich. The Austrian Army had ceased to exist, and many officers were replaced by Prussians. Gauleiter Bürckel of the Saarland was installed as head of the Austrian Nazi Party. His job was to organize the coming election which was 'overwhelmingly' to vote for the new regime.

On 28th March Göring made a speech addressed to the citizens of Vienna. It could not truly be called a German city, he said, so long as it was a city of 300,000 Jews (it also had 400,000 Czechs). Vienna had an important German mission in the field of culture as well as of economics. One thing the Jew must understand clearly and at once: he must get out. According to a US Embassy report, this received the greatest applause of the evening. Meanwhile Dr Ernst Kaltenbrunner, Gestapo and Security Service chief, set up his headquarters at the Rothschild house in the Theresianumgasse. First, however, the entire art collection had to be removed. Under pressure from Gauleiter Bürckel, Louis de Rothschild was forced to sign an agreement to its removal in return for his brother's release from Dachau and safe conduct for them both out of the country. With one stroke of the pen Hitler had acquired one of the most valuable art collections in Austria.

Other Jewish collections were being confiscated and taken to the Hofburg for Hitler and Göring to examine. Bormann had issued strict instructions to Bürckel to keep the confiscations secret. Austrian art experts were ordered to make inventories of all confiscated works of art stored at the special depot in the Hofburg. Lists of the most valuable collections had already been prepared. It then had to be decided under what legal pretext these could be acquired.

The Vienna Kunsthistorisches Museum had one of the finest and most valuable art collections in the world. The museum authorities, devoted to their work, unsympathetic to the new bosses, and forewarned by what had happened earlier in Germany, took evasive action. They had heard about Hitler's ambition to make Munich the greatest art centre, and also that he was considering adding further valuable paintings to the Linz Museum. In an interview with one of the staff I learned that some of the fifteenth- and sixteenth-century masterpieces were removed and put into wooden crates in a special depository, among these Brueghels as well as Cranachs – the great German painter Lucas Cranach was favoured by both Hitler and Göring. Interestingly enough, the crates had been used to store the same pictures during the 1914–18 war, and therefore the same secret identification numbers could be retained in the museum's files. Only a few of the initiated would recognize them and appreciate their significance. When the members of the German art commission swaggered in to inspect the museum's contents they remarked that they were disappointed by the much-lauded exhibits; Berlin had far better paintings. Smilingly the Viennese saw the Germans off the premises, and they were not bothered again.

The round-up of works of art confiscated from private collections in Vienna paid off handsomely for the Nazis. Out of 269 valuable paintings, 122 were earmarked for the Führer's consideration. Göring meanwhile managed to acquire for his own horde two important paintings from the famous collection of the Polish Count Lanckoronski. When Hitler heard about this he reprimanded the Reichsmarschall and demanded the return of the pictures. But Göring never did return them and, undaunted, was now pursuing a painting from the Academy of Fine Arts Museum. For some time the authorities at the Academy hedged. When Göring became more insistent they told him courteously that the official responsible for this particular picture was away on business in Berlin; the matter would have to wait. This time Austrian officialdom was able to defeat the Nazi art vulture, for he was anxious to keep the matter quiet. Perhaps he forgot about the painting; anyway it never left the Academy.

To forestall any further private negotiations of this kind, Hitler issued an order that all Austrian art treasures must remain in the Ostmark (as Austria was renamed by Hitler). It was permitted, however, to buy works of art outright. One picture that Hitler himself was very anxious to acquire was a Vermeer, *The Artist in His Studio*, owned by Count Czernin, who was most reluctant to sell it. It could not be regarded as the property of an enemy of the State, as the Nazis termed it, for the Czernins were Aryan and old-established Austrian aristocrats. However, it appears that pressure was brought to bear on Count Czernin, and for the sum of 1,600,000 Reichsmarks the picture changed hands.

Austria was annexed in March 1938, and already, by the middle of August of that year, Himmler was able to make a detailed list of the private confiscations: 163 of them, worth 93 billion Reichsmarks, the property of the Habsburg family, the Patriotic Front, and the State police. The works of art listed in the so-called Vienna Album were mostly from the Rothschild collection, the balance coming from smaller collections such as Max Reinhardt's.* In the reports these are not regarded as sequestrated

---

* Max Reinhardt (1873–1943), the Austrian actor and stage director, had an important influence in world theatre, founding the world-famous Salzburg Festival in 1920. He left Germany in 1933 when Hitler came to power and went to the United States, where he remained and directed films. He died in the States.

but merely 'secured'. It should be noted that Hitler's art emissaries always 'secured' the art treasures first, and then made further demands which invariably resulted in a decree confiscating the lot, thus lending a kind of legal status to the operation. But on the whole Austria's art treasures were saved from further spoliation partly by Hitler's decree that they should not be taken out of the country, and partly by the actual outbreak of war.

By 1939 war was becoming more and more imminent, and in June of that year the museum authorities in Vienna, having received information that museum staff in Poland were storing their art treasures in safe hiding-places, decided to take their own precautions. They had the most valuable items transported to safe places in the country, keeping the less valuable ones in their own depositories and leaving the least valuable of all on display. Monastery buildings at Melk and Gaming were made available and works of art from the Albertina Museum were sent there. The imperial crown of Austria, the historic collection of coins, and all the jewels from the Hofburg were deposited in the requisitioned Rothschild castle at Stambach. All these precautions were taken in the full knowledge of the Führer.

With the Allied advance and the progressive defeat of the German armies all these treasures were removed to the salt-mines at Laufen, near Salzburg. Stored there too was the entire collection of Vienna's Prince Liechtenstein Gallery. A central heating system was installed in the mine, to prevent the paintings being spoiled by damp. The crown of Charlemagne, which had been housed in the Imperial Treasury, had a different fate, however – or so I was told. Hitler insisted that its rightful place was in Nuremberg in Bavaria, whence it had been taken to Vienna in 1800 for safe keeping. Therefore – despite Austrian protests – it was now removed and lodged at Nuremberg, together with the coronation cloak and regalia.

CHAPTER SIX

Special Mission Linz

It has been said that Hitler was the world's greatest art looter, but in fact Napoleon, who assembled half the world's art treasures in the Louvre, outstripped him. Throughout history the looting of works of art has been accepted as part of the spoils of war. In the days of the Greeks and Romans a defeated nation was always stripped of its treasures. The Romans were especially adept at this practice, and the historian Livy kept records of their booty. The famous bronze horses on the Church of San Marco in Venice were originally plundered from Greece by Julius Caesar and had been mounted on triumphal arches. The Emperor Constantine, setting up the capital of the Byzantine Empire at Constantinople, had the horses removed there. After the city was sacked in 1214 and looted by the Crusaders the horses were taken to Venice, where they have remained ever since. The marble zimborium inside the church, the sculptures on the exterior, and the church's manuscripts, are all part of the loot. A contemporary writer claimed that never had a city benefited so much from plunder.

Over the centuries the pilfering of art treasures by victorious nations became common. During the seventeenth century a more refined method was adopted: the great royal collections (museums did not exist at the time) were purchased rather than stolen. When the Tsarist armies occupied Berlin in 1757 the collection of Frederick II was not touched; to have tampered with it would have been regarded as barbarian even by the Russians. But during the French Revolution everything belonging to the Church and the aristocracy became the property of the nation, and many art treasures and religious sculptures were simply destroyed by the mob. It was several years before the Revolutionary Council appointed an art commissioner empowered to confiscate works of art in the conquered Low Countries and bring them to Paris. The only city spared was Amsterdam, and its royal collection became pretty well the foundation of the present Rijksmuseum. As the French armies advanced into Germany they took from Aachen every item associated with Charlemagne – but not Old Masters, which did not interest them.

It was the young Bonaparte himself who organized the looting. He created an army of commissioners – a sort of fine arts commission – whose job it was to locate and take note of all valuable art treasures. When he became First Consul of France he ordered twenty-two museums to be built. He appointed a supervisor of all French museums, Dominique Vivant Denon, a former diplomat, whose task was to find art treasures that would make the Louvre the greatest art centre in the world. When Napoleon conquered Italy and occupied Venice he helped himself to the Venetian loot. He had the four horses from San Marco dismantled and shipped to Paris to adorn his triumphal carousel. With them, among other valuables, went the bronze lion from the Piazza San Marco. On returning from the triumphs of his Italian campaign Napoleon was entertained by his government and 700 invited guests in the Louvre, on the walls of which were the looted paintings from Holland and Italy. As more loot arrived, 500 sculptures were paraded on chariots down the Champs de Mars in Paris. They were brought to Napoleon in an official presentation.

When the French occupied Berlin in 1806 over a hundred paintings and the great coin collection were shipped to Paris. Other German cities suffered similar confiscations. From Danzig came the Memling altar-piece. Napoleon's brother Joseph, created King of Spain as well as being Napoleon's general, helped himself generously to Spanish art treasures. All these thefts were carried out in the most polite and civilized way; everything taken was catalogued and exchanged for an official receipt.

By 1812 the Louvre had acquired a world-wide reputation as a great art centre, which people from all over the world came to admire. After the fall of Napoleon, however, the looted art treasures had to be packed up and returned to their original owners – including the horses of San Marco. But much that had been taken from private collections was never returned and remained in the Louvre.

During World War I, no doubt with Napoleon's activities in mind, all the belligerent nations appointed officials to protect art treasures. Not so, unfortunately, in World War II. For his plundering activities Hitler took a leaf out of Napoleon's book, but he ignored the finer points of confiscation and kept his activities secret. Pursuing a modernized version of Napoleon's looting tactics, he had by 1940 evolved a complete organization of his own. Under Alfred Rosenberg's direction, it was called Einsatzstab-Reichsleiter Rosenberg – the ERR. And everything was directed towards the building up of the 'Führermuseum' – though in effect it would have been but a pale imitation of Napoleon's great conception of the Louvre. The idea had already come to Hitler by 1938. In that year, after the annexation of Austria, Hitler visited Mussolini in Italy to discuss the situation in South Tyrol and future plans. Among other places, Hitler was shown over the Uffizi and Pitti Galleries in Florence. These great collections of Italian art impressed him immensely and it was these that made him decide to build up a showpiece of German art. In his younger days he had always day-dreamed about replacing cosmopolitan Vienna with a new art centre, and what place could be better for a major gallery than his home town of Linz? He discussed the idea with Albert Speer, his chief architect since Troost's death. He would create a 'supermuseum'; Linz would become an artistic Mecca on the banks of the Danube, to which Vienna would have to take second place. He named the project Sonderauftrag Linz (Special Mission Linz). It was given Top Secret status and was known only to his closest associates and those involved in carrying it out. And not only would he have the museum built, he would re-create Linz itself on the basis of his youthful sketches. This would be the fulfilment of his early dreams of becoming an artist: he had failed then, but now he had the powers of a dictator and his visions of a new Linz could become reality.

Hitler had already surrounded himself with experienced and talented architects to carry out his building plans in Berlin, Nuremberg and Munich. He had discussed expanding the Linz Museum as it then existed with the curator, Professor Kerschner, suggesting that his own private collection should form the nucleus of the new gallery. Haberstock, Hitler's personal art dealer, must have advised that he select an expert to choose paintings for the new centre. The only person suitable for such a project was a Dr Hans Posse, director of the Dresden Art Gallery. Hitler agreed to engage him, only to learn that he had been dismissed by the local Gauleiter, Münschmann, for anti-Nazi sympathies. Hitler, it seems, left immediately for Dresden to give the stunned Gauleiter a dressing-down, and Posse was reinstated in his job.

After meeting Posse, Hitler was so impressed by his expertise that he told him there and then about his Top Secret project for Linz. He wanted Posse to be in charge of setting up the gallery. He knew about his anti-Nazi attitude but needed an expert and not a Party member. Posse was delighted with this sudden turn of events and enthusiastically set about tackling his new job, having been sworn to secrecy. Before long he realized that Hitler knew very little about art. Hitler had always relied on his court photographer, 'Professor' Hoffmann, for advice; but Hoffmann came from the same petty-bourgeois background as his boss and was very limited in his tastes, and consequently the Führer's collection was mediocre.

Posse was determined to make a success of the Linz Museum. It was to be more than just a centre for Bavarian painting: it was to take in important European works as well. Plans were drawn up and architects appointed by Hitler. Speer had the overall super-vision. Now a new phase started in the search for paintings. Waldmüller, Makart, Spitzweg, Lenbach – all German painters of the nineteenth and twentieth centuries – were the nucleus of the new centre but were insufficiently representative of European art. Methods of acquiring other paintings had to be found. Posse went to Vienna, where valuable private collections that had been con-fiscated were assembled at the Hofburg, and from these he made a careful selection. From the Oskar Bondy collection, which con-tained 1,500 items, he earmarked 324. From the Rothschilds' 269 valuable works of art he put aside 122 for Linz. A printed catalogue had even been produced listing the twelve confiscated collections, and from this Posse compiled his own list which he sent, via Bormann, to Hitler for his consideration. The remainder was to be distributed to Austrian museums and galleries.

Hitler then turned his sights on Czechoslovakia, whose people he had heartily loathed during his years in Vienna (it was always said that more Czechs lived in Vienna than in their own capital, Prague). After the Nazi take-over of Czechoslovakia in 1939

Hitler stayed briefly at the Hradchin Castle in Prague, historic seat of the kings of Bohemia and furnished with many art treasures. When he went back to Germany six valuable Gobelin tapestries went too. The castles of Czechoslovakia provided some wonderful private collections of armoury from the Middle Ages. All the Czech loot, too, was carefully recorded, packed and dispatched – earmarked for the Führermuseum – to the depository at Munich. Yet the Czech museums did not fare too badly, as Hitler was not interested in Bohemian art – he considered it Slav, and therefore inferior, art.

Meanwhile the architects were planning the new Linz, based on Hitler's sketches. Though war was now imminent, Hitler always found time to discuss his beloved Linz project. Now all-powerful leader of the German Reich, he expected to conquer Europe, perhaps the world. Yet if Fate had not destined him for this role, he was often to remark to associates, he would himself have become an architect and a second Michelangelo. He was already showing his preoccupation with architecture by 1933; Vienna, with its magnificent buildings, had left its impression on him. In Munich he had had his architect Troost remodel the Braune Haus, the Nazi headquarters, for him. Now as Führer he could put his ideas into practice, order the construction of impressive buildings, and redesign major German cities. Albert Speer, Troost's successor, describes vividly in *Inside the Third Reich* how Berlin, Munich and Nuremberg were all transformed by new buildings and wide boulevards. The might of the Third Reich had to be housed magnificently, and Hitler knew full well how to stage manage his public appearances, especially at Party rallies and at the vast Olympic Stadium. The outbreak of war ensured that much of the new building programme never got beyond the stage of architectural models. Nevertheless to the end Hitler believed that the work would be finished.

He seems to have been fascinated by domed buildings. In Vienna, churches, theatres and museums have particularly impressive domes and this may have influenced him. He also liked to include tall columns in the design wherever possible. His own final resting-place, designed by Herman Giesler after Hitler's own plan, was to have been a domed mausoleum adjoining the Braune Haus.

CHAPTER SEVEN

The Rape of Poland

Forewarned by the annexation of Czechoslovakia and benefiting from the temporary peace gained by the British prime minister, Neville Chamberlain, museum curators in Poland were taking their own precautions. As has been noted earlier, they had their most valuable works of art crated and stored. No one apart from Hitler and his closest henchmen, however, could have realized quite how near war was. On 3rd September, 1939 Hitler's armies invaded Poland and within a few weeks the entire country was under occupation. Hitler's aim was the total destruction of the Polish nation and Polish culture.

In the wake of the victorious Wehrmacht came the art vultures. No finesse was to be shown (aside from the capricious handing over of receipts, referred to later), even though the Polish museum authorities had established friendly relations with the Ost Europa Institut (East Europe Institute). This had been established by the Nazis as a so-called research centre for Eastern European cultural affairs. Its members would pay frequent visits to Poland and visit museums and art collections to compare notes with the museum curators – all purely for research purposes, of course. The museum authorities in Cracow could not believe their eyes when the eminent German art historian, Professor Frey, who had visited them so often, turned up in SS uniform. Together with a Gestapo colleague, he headed the Nazi art commission which then visited the Warsaw Museum. The institute proved to have been concerned only with locating art treasures in Eastern Europe in anticipation of the take-over. Clearly its members had been prepared for this function long before the war broke out and were working to a set plan. They had full lists of Polish works of art, compiled by the German art historians on their earlier visits. This was confirmed indirectly to me in 1965 by the former curator of the coin collection in the Kunsthistorisches Museum in Vienna, appointed by Hitler to take charge of this section of the Linz Museum. They had had prior information, he told me, about the Poles having put their art treasures in safe keeping.

An Austrian Nazi with the rank of SS Colonel, Dr Katejan Mühlmann, was appointed by Göring in October 1939 to 'secure' all Polish-owned art treasures – despite the Hague Convention, which Nazi Germany had ratified. Regulation 1907, article 46 of the Hague Convention declares that family honour and rights, the lives of persons, private property, as well as religious convictions and practice, must be respected. Private property cannot be confiscated, and in article 47 pillage is formally forbidden. Moreover, article 56 states that the property of municipalities, as well as that of institutions dedicated to religion, charity and education or the arts and sciences, even if belonging to the State, shall be treated as private property. All seizure of, destruction or wilful damage done to institutions of this character, historic monuments, works of art and science, is forbidden but, should it occur, it is subject to legal proceedings. This was blatantly ignored by the Nazi commission when, with the help of Himmler's SS, they carried out their work of plunder.

Warsaw was treated more harshly than Cracow because it resisted German attacks by dive-bombers and artillery for longer. The royal castle in Warsaw, with its treasures from the days of the Polish kings, suffered considerable damage to the roof, and its ballroom was destroyed. The curator gave instructions for repairs to be carried out, but this work was stopped by the Germans. Art experts from Vienna and Breslau took over and began to sort out the works of art, most of which had been crated ready to be taken to places of safety. Orders went out that all State, ecclesiastical and private treasures were to be confiscated. Everything was to be assembled in Cracow. Professor Frey's first task on arrival in Warsaw was to locate the twenty-five Canaletto paintings that had been taken from the castle to the museum's depository. They were immediately earmarked for sending to Germany. When the new governor-general of Poland, Hans Frank, visited the castle, he strode up to the canopy that covered the royal throne and tore off the silver embroidered eagles, emblem of Poland, to keep as souvenirs. A systematic dismantling of all movable objects took place in the royal castle in Warsaw. In the Middle Ages the Polish kings had engaged Saxon artists to build and decorate the castle. The Nazis therefore maintained that, as it was of German origin, it was their rightful property.

Elsewhere in Poland, confiscations were being systematically carried out. The National Museum in Cracow, the private collections of Polish aristocrats, and in particular the churches and monasteries, all were stripped of their works of art. From the Church of Our Lady in Cracow, Gothic and Baroque chalices were taken.

Once the first collection of looted treasures had been gathered together, Dr Posse, who as already noted was in charge of the proposed Linz Museum, arrived in Poland for an inspection. His report to Berlin makes interesting reading. He pointed out, first of all, that it was difficult for him to get a clear idea of how to dispose of the confiscated works of art, as most were packed in crates and stored in Cracow and Warsaw. He reported that box cars of them were arriving daily at the Cracow depot from public, ecclesiastical and private sources, that all items were being photographed, and that Frank, as governor-general of Poland, would be sending the Führer an album of photographs for selection. He advised that Germany couldn't hope to enrich herself with great works of art from Poland, with the exception of the 'Veit Stoss', known in Poland as Wit Stwosz, an altar-piece from Cracow's Church of Our Lady. This world-famous Gothic triptych was carved by the Nuremberg artist Veit Stoss, commissioned by the King of Poland in 1477, and took ten years to complete. The centre of the triptych shows the Virgin asleep, surrounded by angels; the side panels show scenes from the lives of Jesus and Mary. The predella (the platform which forms the base) shows the genealogy of Christ. (The altar-piece was in fact taken to Nuremberg, and was found there after the war inadequately stored in a bunker.) From the same church the Nazis took nine paintings, dated 1515, by Hans von Kulmbach, one of Dürer's best pupils. Once again they claimed German ownership because of the artist's nationality.

Dr Posse referred also to Raphael's *Portrait of a Young Man*, a Rubens *Landscape*, and Leonardo da Vinci's *Lady with a Weasel*. The latter work was painted for the Duke of Milan, Lodovico Sforza ('Il Moro') in 1483, and is said to be the portrait of his mistress, Cecilia Galleriani. Posse went on to mention the Czartoryski Museum collection as being of interest. This had been one of the first private museums in Europe and contained many art treasures. The pictures, Posse indicated, had already gone to Berlin, but he was interested in some of the above items for Linz.

In his report Posse noted the stripping of the royal castle in Warsaw. All the panelling, doors, inlaid floors, sculptures, mirrors, chandeliers and porcelain was to be taken out and taken to Germany for use in the pavilion of the Zwinger Palace in Dresden. This work was eventually carried out, but so crudely – the Gestapo used unskilled Jewish prisoners for the work – that most of what was dismantled was destroyed in the process. Parquet flooring was ripped up with pickaxes, panelling forcibly levered off, sculptures knocked down, and the whole lot piled into trucks with no protection against bad weather. Only a few bits and pieces were secreted away by the Polish officials.*

In addition, Posse's report mentioned the *Blood Banner of the Prophet*, which he believed had been removed by the Russians when in occupation of their zone after the signing of the German-Soviet Pact. He also mentioned some Dürer engravings, thought to have been taken by the Russians from Lvov. These did not come to light until the Germans entered Lvov in their drive towards Russia. The curator of the Bawarowski Museum, it appeared, had hidden them, though at first he denied all knowledge of their whereabouts. He gave way under pressure from the Gestapo, and the engravings were at once confiscated in return for a receipt, the thirty-one engravings being sent to Göring, who in turn passed them on to Hitler. Hitler was so

---

* After it had been stripped, the castle was occupied for a time by the military. Finally, it was blown up. A detailed account of the destruction of the royal castle is given in *The Nazi Culture in Europe* (H.M. Stationery Office, 1945).

pleased with them that he had them hung at his headquarters.

This issuing of receipts – in effect quite worthless – was always the Nazi's justification when 'safeguarding' works of art. It came up continually in the discussions I had with Germans who clearly still had Nazi sympathies. Objects had certainly been taken, they would argue, but not without a receipt. One ex-Wehrmacht officer complained to me about his watch having been taken by Allied troops when he was a prisoner. I remarked that the Germans had done the same thing, and worse. 'But we gave signed receipts!' he said.

It is clear from Posse's report that for the Linz project itself Poland did not provide any great pickings, beyond a few Old Masters and the Veit Stoss altar-piece. Hitler was contemptuous of all the Slav nations and would not have wanted Polish paintings in his centre of Germanic art. For his occupying forces, however, it was quite otherwise. As well as pictures, Poland had a rich collection of *objets d'art*: tapestries, bronzes, coins, armour, porcelain, antique furniture, manuscripts, antiquarian books had all been sought after by Polish collectors. The German invaders helped themselves liberally to these riches. Much of the loot was sent to Germany so that high-ranking Nazis could take their pick.

Mühlmann, to curry favour with Reichsmarschall Göring, pilfered Watteau's *The Pretty Polish Girl* and sent it to Karinhall. Governor Frank was presented by the appreciative Gestapo with Rembrandt's *Portrait of a Young Man* from the royal Lazienski collection. Frank himself took a choice collection of treasures for his two residences in Poland, the royal castle in Cracow and Kressendorf Castle. When he was picked up by US Army units at the end of the war, his Bavarian country house was also found to be stacked with loot from Poland. Among it was Bernardo Belotto's *Cracow Suburbs*. Belotto, pupil of his more famous uncle Canaletto, settled in Warsaw in 1767 and worked there till the end of his life for King Stanislas Poniatowski. His contemporary views of Warsaw are topographically very exact and were used, after World War II, to help rebuild the old part of the city just as it had been before its destruction by the Nazis. These views of Warsaw were also the first paintings Frey chose to send back to Germany on his arrival. After the war they were returned unharmed to Poland.

The official Polish document, *Warsaw Accuses*, published in

1945, gives harrowing details of the deliberate destruction of the royal castle and subsequently of many other historic buildings during the Nazi retreat, a final piece of vandalistic revenge by the Nazis after they had removed the remaining works of art from museums and libraries to Germany. A secret inventory was kept by the Warsaw museum authorities which revealed the extent of the confiscations from Warsaw alone: 2,774 paintings of the European school, 10,738 Polish paintings from the sixteenth to twentieth century, 1,379 scupltures. After the suppression of the uprising under General Bor the remaining contents of the Warsaw museums, according to official sources, were systematically pilfered. Wanton destruction soon took hold. Paintings and sculptures were smashed or shot at. Limoges enamels of the Renaissance were used to eat off and then thrown away. Gobelin tapestries were cut up and used as blankets. Those members of the armed forces who did have some appreciation of the arts took what they liked and sent it home through the military field post. Nothing remained of the deliberately destroyed royal castle but a corner of the wall. The cathedral suffered the same fate. Priceless monuments of the sixteenth and seventeenth centuries, among them the tombs of the princes of Masovia, were turned to rubble. Systematic destruction of churches and palaces was carried out under the supervision of the SS general, Geibel. The Palace of Lazienski with its paintings and its beautiful ceilings by Bacciarelli was burned. As the Germans retreated before the advancing Russian Army, libraries full of historical manuscripts and archives went up in flames, the National Museum was mined, and the remains of its collection was driven off in trucks to the Reich. The royal collection of paintings which had been secreted away was discovered and taken.

Of all the works of art that were looted from Poland the greatest single loss was Raphael's *Portrait of a Young Man*, taken from the Czartoryski Gallery in Cracow. It was sent to Berlin, earmarked for the Linz Museum, but then disappeared. According to one report, the three pictures that Posse specifically chose for Linz were rejected by Hitler and returned to Governor Frank in Cracow. One of them, Leonardo's *Lady with a Weasel*, was recovered from his home in Bavaria. What happened to the Raphael painting, however, is not known. It may be either hidden somewhere or, as has so often happened, be in the possession of someone who does not know its value. Other serious losses were Rubens's *Christ Carrying the Cross* and Guardi's *Venetian Palace*, both from the Warsaw National Museum.

Hitler had originally intended to send the remainder of the treasures stored in Cracow to Königsberg, in East Prussia, where a museum was to be built. Göring had given the order for this as the Soviet armies advanced on Poland. But much of it never reached its destination; some was found in Bavaria, but some disappeared completely. A good deal of the loot was recovered after the war from the homes of Nazi leaders who had been stationed in Poland. But in the aftermath of the war a huge number of looted treasures changed hands and could never be traced. Today there may be treasures from Poland in the possession of collectors who bought them quite legitimately, ignorant of their origin.

CHAPTER EIGHT

Designs on France
and the Low Countries

To the Allied countries it seemed that the 'phoney war' or *Sitzkrieg* could last indefinitely; but in May and June 1940 Hitler moved in on Holland, Belgium, Luxembourg and France. Here he decided to tread more carefully. For the time being the emissaries of Special Mission Linz were to slow down their 'safeguarding' operations. In a secret order issued by the German High Command to all military commanders it was decreed that the occupying armies should treat the populations of these countries with consideration; the Hague Convention was to be adhered to and normal economic life to be maintained. Consequently the unrestrained looting of Poland was not repeated, and the German Army established its own *Kunstschutz* (Fine Arts Protection) mission which operated in the newly occupied territories in accordance with the Hague Convention. It was not informed, however, of Hitler's ultimate intentions.

Shortly after France's surrender had been signed in Compiègne on 22nd June, 1940, Hitler flew to Paris for an early morning art tour of the city. In his book *Inside the Third Reich* Albert Speer relates how he arrived at Le Bourget at 5.30 am on 28th June,

1940. Hitler, Speer, Giesler (architect for Munich and Linz), and Arno Breker the sculptor climbed into waiting Mercedes cars and toured Paris. Hitler was especially impressed by the Opéra, by Napoleon's tomb at Les Invalides, the Panthéon, and the Church of the Sacré Coeur which dominates the Paris skyline from Montmartre. There he lingered for quite a time as the church-goers went in. To Breker, who had studied in Paris, he remarked that he too would have come to study there if he had not been destined for a political career.

Hitler told Speer afterwards that this short visit to Paris had been the fulfilment of his life's dream. The beauty of the city had deeply impressed him, but he considered that the new Berlin he was planning would outshine Paris. He might, he thought, even have to destroy Paris, the way he had destroyed Warsaw – the city he would not allow to be rebuilt because he wanted to deprive the Poles of their cultural capital. To Speer it was incomprehensible that Hitler could even toy with the idea of destroying the most beautiful city in Europe. Yet if Paris had not been declared an open city in the last days of the fighting by the commander of the German troops, it might well have been obliterated.

To find out how the Kunstschutz had operated I went in search of someone who had been attached to it. I had little luck with German official sources, but was told in Paris that a Count Wolff Metternich had been in charge. When I tracked him down at his home at Bad Godesberg, a spa near Bonn, I found a charming elderly gentleman from an old Rhineland family. He seemed very pleased to be interviewed, especially as the looting of works of art had sometimes been unfairly blamed on the German Army. As an eminent scholar and curator of the Rhineland museums, he had been appointed by General Wagner to the Kunstschutz with the rank of colonel, and entrusted with the protection of the fine arts in France, Belgium, Holland and Luxembourg. He was known to the French museum authorities, and in particular for his anti-Nazi sympathies – one of the reasons he had been put in charge of the mission.

Wagner's division (Wagner was executed subsequently for being involved in the plot on Hitler's life) came under the command of General von Brauchitsch. The Kunstschutz units had been rapidly organized by the army High Command to forestall a repetition of what had happened in Poland. Von

Brauchitsch, at the head of all the occupying armies, at once put all museums and depositories of art out of bounds to troops and Nazi personnel. Wolff Metternich arrived in Paris with his assistant von Tischowitz and was installed in the Hôtel Majestic.

'Our unit was ordered to act in accordance with the Hague Convention, to which Germany had been a signatory,' Count Wolff Metternich told me. 'Our activity was strictly limited to those countries where a military administration had been established – France, Belgium, the Netherlands, Greece and Yugoslavia. In France, all the museums had evacuated their collections in 1939 to various châteaux and other buildings throughout the countryside. This complex operation had been organized by the French national museums under the direction of Monsieur Jeujard, director of the State museums in Paris.'

The Bayeux Tapestry and other art treasures were evacuated from Paris before the Germans reached it and distributed around the countryside. Count Wolff Metternich was given a list of 350,000 works of art from the Louvre and other French museums. He had all the places where works of art were stored put under military guard as soon as he arrived, he told me. Lists were carefully drawn up in co-operation with the French authorities as a means of checking subsequently as to whether any item had been removed. Meanwhile the German commander-in-chief, Field-Marshal Wilhelm Keitel, issued an order to the governor of Paris, General von Böckelberg, regarding the 'safeguarding' of works of art belonging to the French nation and to individual Jews. 'This measure did not constitute an expropriation, but only a transfer into German custody as a pawn in the final peace negotiations,' it was stated.

The intention, clearly, was to induce a false sense of security; Keitel must have been told by Hitler what he had in mind. Already it had been reported to Count Wolff Metternich that the Gestapo had entered private homes and sequestrated works of art in the absence of the Jewish owners. Inventories were made and the premises sealed off. Jews had been declared by Hitler to be outlaws, irrespective of their nationality, and consequently the Hague Convention did not apply to them.

A further sign of what was in store was the arrival at the German Embassy in Paris of a Baron von Künsberg, an emissary from Ribbentrop. His job was to make an inventory of all the

French national collections and to select the best pieces for transfer to an assembly point. After detailed inspection certain works of art were to be selected for presentation by the French people to the Führer. Assisting him was a certain German art connoisseur who had lived in Paris for fifteen years and knew exactly what was on the art market as well as in the French museums. He was attached to the Künsberg mission as artistic adviser.

'I was able to circumvent this plan,' Count Wolff Metternich informed me. 'I got von Brauchitsch to issue me with a new order protecting all the art depots. Nobody could enter without von Brauchitsch's personally signed authorization. At the same time I had all the châteaux and historic houses – about 500 in all – put out of bounds to German troops. These measures eventually led to a break between the army and the Party authorities, and I was reported by von Künsberg to Hitler for my anti-Nazi attitude, but curiously enough no measures were taken against me. I think the Nazis must have feared that their secret plans would be exposed if there were a scandal.'

Meanwhile into the Jeu de Paume Museum in the Tuileries gardens were flowing valuable works of art confiscated from wealthy French Jews such as the Rothschilds, Kahns, Levy de Benzion, Seligmann, the celebrated art dealer, and many others. The Rosenberg task force, the ERR, prepared lists of the whereabouts of all confiscated works, supplied by informers from the Paris art world.

The Musée de l'Armée, housed in the Hôtel des Invalides, was never evacuated to a safe place, since it came under the jurisdiction of the Ministry of War. The Germans went to great trouble to compile a list of 2,000 objects in it that were of German origin and had been taken as booty by Napoleon, including also relics from the Franco-Prussian War and World War I. Returning to Paris as victors, the Germans considered they had the right to reclaim these trophies. The 2,000 items were dispatched back to Germany for the enrichment of German military science and Prussian militarism. This proved to be but a temporary move, for after Hitler's defeat they were restored to the Musée de l'Armée.

Hitler showed great respect, however, for Napoleon's tomb in Les Invàlides. He even gave instructions that the remains of Napoleon's son, the Duke of Reichstadt, be brought from Vienna to be placed beside his father's tomb. A guidebook in German was to have been produced for the edification of visiting German soldiers, but in the event it was never printed.

The Louvre reopened in the autumn of 1940, with its most valuable treasures stored in one of the châteaux of the Loire in the Vichy zone, out of bounds to looters. During all this time French artists were in no way prevented from working and selling their work. In fact, they were encouraged to continue pursuing these activities, so that the Germans stationed in Paris might have souvenirs to send home. Goebbels even arranged sponsored visits to Berlin for French artists, where they received VIP treatment. But many refused the offer, realizing it was part of a propaganda effort to stress Franco-German 'artistic amity'. The French public was amused when the German sculptor Breker was sent by Goebbels to Paris to exhibit his muscular male nudes and gigantic horses.

Between 1940 and 1942 life in Paris was easy-going for the German occupying forces and the various Nazi organizations centred there. However, after a time things were tightened up, and as a result overstaffed offices and high living among the bosses became a thing of the past. For the ERR this was a cause of much dissatisfaction, especially to Colonel von Behr of the Amt West, which was separate from ERR itself. Von Behr was regarded as a high-handed dandy, and was disliked for his ruthless attitude to his staff. He entertained the top brass lavishly, although he was merely attached to the Red Cross army group. He had been installed by Göring, and was responsible for Göring's train transports to Germany.

High in the German military administration in Paris there was another of Göring's agents. He combined forces with a police officer of the Sûreté and a former woman employee of the Seligmann Art Gallery to uncover works of art hidden by Jewish owners and compile lists for confiscation. When General von Stülpnagel, Commander-in-Chief of the Wehrmacht, heard about this the official was recalled to Berlin – much to Göring's annoyance. But the setback by no means deterred the Reichsmarschall from acquiring the works of art he wanted for Karinhall. At the suggestion of his buyer, Andreas Hofer, he arranged for two French-Jewish dealer brothers to be 'aryanized', and in return for gaining his protection they offered him a valuable present. This he refused to accept, but he did do an exchange deal with them for some paintings confiscated by the ERR. The brothers' gallery in Paris became the meeting-place for art dealer collaborators.

By the autumn of 1940 Paris was teeming with dealers from all over Germany. The Paris art market now had much to offer. Hitler's own buyer, Haberstock, would announce his impending arrival by inserting a notice in the *Gazette des Beaux Arts*, thus alerting his various French dealer friends to visit him at his usual haunt, the Ritz. Among other paintings, Haberstock purchased Veronese's *Leda and the Swan* and Teniers's *Scene from Family Life*. Money seemed to be no object to him. For the Etienne Nicolas collection he paid 1,800,000 francs; while for seven paintings – among them *Rivoli* by Gustave Courbet, the leading French realist painter of the nineteenth century – he paid 930,000 francs. Another very active dealer, a competitor for Haberstock, was a Frau Dietrich from Munich, who had already sold many pictures intended for Linz through her friend Heinrich Hoffmann, Hitler's photographer and art adviser. Like the other official Nazi buyers she had a special VIP pass which enabled her to travel outside Germany. Bormann, who controlled all foreign exchange permits, had allocated sufficient funds for her to buy for the Linz collection. She saw over 270 paintings and bought eighty.

All these acquisitions were dispatched to Munich to the Führer's headquarters, the Führerbau. Here Hitler held regular inspections, relying greatly on Dr Posse's advice as to what should be selected for Linz. The rejects went back to the dealer, who could then sell in the open market. As all his buyers worked on a commission basis Hitler was never the loser himself. Once an object had been chosen the dealer was promptly paid by Hans Lammers, head of the Treasury, who held the purse-strings for the Linz project. Frau Dietrich could always sell rejects, as she had most of the top Nazis as her clients. Bormann also bought from her for the Treasury at Berlin.

During the Occupation the art market both in France and Holland became cut-throat in its dealings. Dealers were not slow to realize that the pickings were good, and most Nazi buyers had little knowledge of art. A good many faked paintings were offered, and sometimes even knowledgeable dealers were taken in. By ruthlessly exploiting the French franc exchange rate at twenty to one in favour of the Reichskassenscheine or invasion mark,

German dealers were assured of 100 per cent profit on their purchases when selling to customers in Germany. Having been paid in French francs, the original purchases were legal; it was the individual seller who eventually suffered the financial loss, not the French State. This system appears to have been deliberately adopted by the Nazi authorities to forestall any future claims for restitution.

With this advantageous exchange rate it is not surprising that nearly fifty German art dealers were competing against one another, often – unknown to each other – for the same client. Many French people who owned paintings and other valuables that had not been affected by ERR confiscations cashed in on the bonanza, though keeping it secret so as not to seem unpatriotic. Nor is it surprising that German museums and galleries had their own experts bidding.

As soon as the ERR had arranged a display of the confiscated Jewish collections in the Jeu de Paume galleries, Göring would arrive with his art dealer Hofer. The Reichsmarschall always came in civilian dress in an endeavour to avoid attracting attention. Puffing at a cigar and refreshing himself from time to time with a glass of champagne thoughtfully provided by the ERR staff, he would spend a considerable time studying the various exhibits. According to Count Wolff Metternich, he was interested mainly in Impressionist and Baroque paintings. On his first visit he chose four pictures. Soon afterwards he assumed overall control of all ERR activities in France, much to the annoyance not only of Rosenberg himself but of Goebbels and even Bormann, who hitherto had kept indirect control over the Paris confiscations. The ERR depended now on Göring for transport and personnel, especially after the commencement of hostilities on the Russian front. In his directive to the chief of the military administration in Paris, as well as the ERR, Göring gave instructions as to the disposal of confiscated works of art. The priorities were as follows: first, works of art about which the Führer wished to make a personal decision; secondly, those destined for the Reichsmarschall's personal collection; thirdly, those destined for centres of higher education; and lastly those destined for museums and galleries. Göring would give von Behr forty-eight hours' notice of his arrival in Paris, in response to which the latest collection of loot would be put on show for him at the Jeu de Paume. He appointed as his Paris representative a young German art expert who specialized in seventeenth-century Dutch paintings. This individual was put into Luftwaffe uniform and accorded an inconspicuous, low rank. Since Hitler relied on Göring to keep him informed of any interesting confiscations for the Linz project, the Reichsmarschall was free to pick and choose as he liked for himself.

After his first visit to Paris in the autumn of 1940 to choose paintings for his collection at Karinhall, Göring decided to clarify his position vis-à-vis Alfred Rosenberg who, from Berlin, controlled the Einsatzstab engaged in confiscating Jewish property in France. In a letter to Rosenberg sent from his hunting-lodge at Rominten at the end of November 1940, Göring established his future relations with the ERR and justified his actions during his recent visits to Paris. He welcomed the establishment of a department responsible for art confiscations in France, he said, but noted that there were others claiming to have the Führer's backing. Foreign Minister Ribbentrop had circulated a letter claiming the right to deal with the 'safeguarding' of art treasures in occupied countries, for example. Having forewarned Rosenberg of internal intrigues, Göring promised full support for the ERR in the form of transport and special uniformed guards. He had advised the Luftwaffe accordingly. From Göring's further statements it is clear that attempts by Jewish art owners to secrete their property in rural hide-outs was not very successful. Using bribery as well as French detectives and informers he had already located many hiding-places, and furthermore the German exchange control authorities, on his instructions, had searched all French bank depositories for valuables.

Göring mentioned his valuable art collection which, with the Führer's approval and support, was to pass to the State on his death on condition it remained at Karinhall. He needed a few more items for his collection from the Jewish confiscations. The evaluation and purchase of each was to be made by an art expert appointed by the French Government, the payments to be made to a trustee appointed by the German Government. The Führer was to be kept informed. Göring seems to have had some scruples about his first acquisitions: out of hundreds of confiscated paintings he had selected only fifteen, he said, which was not very many considering he had been responsible for discovering the hide-outs. Of the most valuable items, the Führer would have first choice. Nevertheless, he added, thousands of works of art should be available for museums and official buildings. His letter, Göring concluded, was for Rosenberg's personal information and was written with the purpose of avoiding any future misunderstandings.

It soon became clear how Göring himself interpreted the remarks made in his letter. He had arranged that the French authorities' official appraiser was a Parisian artist who was favourably inclined towards the Reichsmarschall. He would value, at the lowest possible market prices, the paintings selected from the auctions at the Jeu de Paume that were organized by the ERR. Thus the sale of confiscated works of art was 'legalized' in the eyes of buyers – and there were many besides Göring. Though the original price would be low, Hofer would always beat it down further. It was in his own interests to do so, as he could make a fortune out of a rejected picture on the Berlin art market. When the deal was concluded he would dispatch the selected pictures to the Reich for payment at a later date by the recipient, but this was always delayed and sometimes never took place. Originally the monies were to have been paid to the French Government and into a fund for the children of French soldiers killed in the war.

The 'King of the Arts' was a former Berlin art historian who had established himself as a dealer in Switzerland in the 1930s and had good connections in the Paris art market. Once the Germans had occupied Paris and the Einsatzstab Rosenberg had begun its confiscations he became a valued middleman. As he remained a civilian he was able to travel to the Midi in search of the many Jewish collectors and dealers who had fled there to escape Gestapo persecution. They were not always able to do so, as became clear in the case of the Schloss collection, an extremely valuable Jewish-owned collection of paintings. When Haberstock was in Nice he was approached by one of the Schloss family, a woman, who offered him some items for sale. Nothing came of the proposal, but Haberstock was interested and got the Vichy authorities to investigate for him. When the value of the collection was realized, pressure was put on the Vichy police by the Gestapo to arrest the Schloss family on some pretext or other, and the collection – mostly Dutch Old Masters – was then confiscated.

After a cloak-and-dagger operation by the Germans the

Roses by Adolf Hitler, dated 1912
Trenches at Douaumont (Verdun) by Adolf Hitler, dated
1914

The old Hofburgtheater, Vienna. *Above* is Hitler's painting of it and *below* the print from which he copied the scene.

The Discus Thrower a
typical example of
approved Nazi art.

(*Left*) Painting by Professor Glaubacher of Hitler on the balcony of the town hall at Linz in 1938.

(*Right*) The Crown of Charlemagne, which was taken by the Nazis from Austria to Nuremberg, where it was recovered at the end of World War II, hidden in an underground bunker.

(*Below right*) Hitler enters Vienna, 1938.

(*Below*) Hitler returns in triumph to his birthplace, Braunau am Inn, on 12th March, 1938.

(*Left and below*) Two models of the Führermuseum planned for Linz.

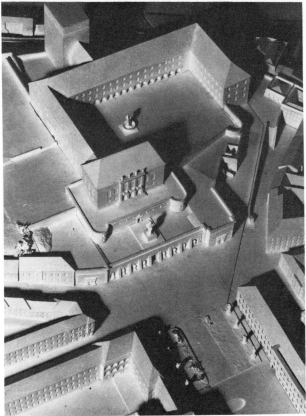

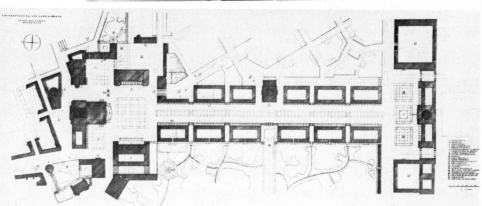

The plans for Linz:
'The European Art Centre' drawn by the architect Roderick Fick. In the centre is the opera house; on the left the museum, with the library opposite; on one side of the opera house is the Bruckner Hall, and on the other the Operetta theatre.

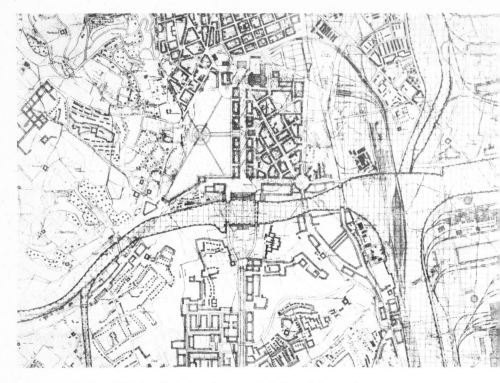

The detailed plans for the rebuilding of the whole town.

The drawing and model of the new railway station. The design by Fick was based on Hitler's ideas.

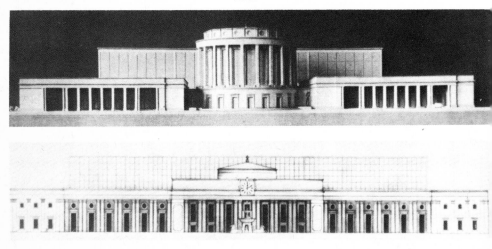

pictures reached Paris. They were exhibited at the Jeu de Paume and sold to two buyers. Dr Voss, on Hitler's behalf, bought 263 pictures, valued at 50 million francs, for the Linz gallery; while the Vichy government, on behalf of the Louvre, bought forty-nine pictures for just under 19 million francs. As far as Hitler was concerned the whole thing was a bad bargain and he was very angry with Voss, reproaching him for the fact that the best items had been bought by the French. The Schloss family were promised payment, but in fact received nothing. After the war, however, they had the satisfaction of having the entire collection returned to them by the French Government.

Nazi efforts to keep the Einsatzstab Rosenberg and its confiscations secret had little success; its activities became all too obvious and led to official repercussions. The German military commander of Paris protested about the fact that the ERR confiscated the Wildenstein collection from the Jeu de Paume and sent it to Germany. This was contrary to Göring's original instructions to respect State property and legal government. But Göring had never officially formulated his instructions in writing, and he himself was the first to infringe them. To avoid confiscation of the rest of the Wildenstein collection, the firm was 'aryanized' under new French ownership.

The ERR was tricked by this clever move, engineered by a German art dealer, and to avoid unwelcome publicity had to accept it as legal. Yet they had arranged to pounce on the valuable works of art deposited by Wildenstein in the Château de Sourches, near Paris. Göring meanwhile was furious that this now non-Jewish concern could sell in the open market without fear of confiscation. A valuable haul had slipped through his fingers.

Himmler too was unsuccessful when he sent agents to try to obtain the famous Bayeux Tapestry, depicting scenes of the Norman Conquest. One local wit suggested that Himmler wanted to study it in order to learn how to invade England.

Between 1941 and 1942 one of Göring's art dealers exchanged eighty modern paintings for Old Masters from Switzerland. Rosenberg reported that his organization had done similar deals with several confiscated modern paintings. Anyone protesting was immediately branded an enemy of the Reich. Among their confiscations from Jewish owners the ERR had expropriated quite a number of 'degenerate' works of art, and as a symbolic gesture a pile of them was stacked up near the Jeu de Paume and burnt. In the dark it was impossible to see exactly what went into the bonfire, but apparently nothing saleable was destroyed.

After the first nine months of the Nazi occupation of France, the ERR compiled a report for Hitler. Under the heading 'Special Mission Linz' confiscations from the Jewish-owned collections of Rothschild, Khan, Seligmann and others were listed. The report affirmed that twenty-five freight cars of valuable paintings, furniture, tapestries, jewellery and *objets d'art* had arrived at the Neuschwanstein Castle depot in Bavaria. It continued as follows: 'These confiscations of the Einsatzstab [ERR] are in accordance, my Führer, with your orders of October 1940 from Paris. With the assistance of the SD [Sicherheitsdienst] and the secret police, we have systematically located the hide-outs containing art objects belonging to Jewish owners who have fled the country, and taken the contents to the Louvre for disposal.'

Every item was carefully recorded and photographed, stated the report, the inventory listing over 4,000 works of art of great value. Two wagonloads of the most important of these, personally selected by Reichsmarschall Göring, had been forwarded to Munich. To unload and display these would take four weeks, after which they would be ready for the Führer's inspection. It would take a further three or four months to round up the remaining Jewish art properties in the western zone, and they would then also be forwarded to Germany. The report was signed by Gerhardt Utikal, who was in charge of the ERR consignments.

At the auctions in the Jeu de Paume works of art that were not earmarked for the Linz project or for Göring were often bought by Nazi officials, German generals, or even French collaborators. The French Government made an official protest to the authorities about the confiscations from Jews, but it had no effect, apart from a reply accusing the French of ingratitude for the altruistic efforts of the ERR in saving invaluable cultural material from loss or destruction. Furthermore, legal justification for the confiscation was claimed. The French were reminded that the Hague Convention rules about private property, which were part of the armistice terms of June 1940 at Compiègne, did not apply to Jews and Freemasons, since the armistice was between the French and the German nations.

The biggest treasure-hunt of World War II involved Belgium's national art treasure, the world-famous Van Eyck altar-piece from the cathedral in Ghent. On the outbreak of hostilities in 1939 the Belgian Government decided to move it to a safer place, as their country would probably be in the front line of battle. They gratefully accepted an offer from the French museum authorities to store it for them at Pau, in the Pyrenees. When France was occupied, Pau was within the zone of the Vichy government and out of the Germans' reach. The director of the French museums had even obtained a written undertaking from the Germans that the altar-piece would not be removed without the written permission of the Mayor of Ghent, the French museum authorities, and the Kunstschutz.

The history of the altar-piece, as Count Wolff Metternich explained to me, goes back to 1432. Known as *The Adoration of the Lamb*, it was painted by the brothers Hubert and Jan van Eyck and consisted of twelve panels. It had been commissioned, it was said, by one of the wealthiest citizens of Ghent and was placed in the town's Cathedral of St Bavon. During the Protestant period in the sixteenth century the polyptych was hidden, being returned to the cathedral when the town became Catholic again. Then in 1781, after the Emperor Joseph II of Bohemia and Austria had expressed distaste for the nudity of Adam and Eve, one of the panels was removed. When Napoleon came to power Ghent was captured by the French, and the four centre panels were taken to the Louvre by Napoleon – curiously, the altar wings were not taken. When Napoleon escaped from Elba, King Louis XVIII fled to Ghent. Then, after Napoleon's final defeat at Waterloo and the King's return to Paris, he sent back the centre panels to Ghent in gratitude.

Some time later, while the Bishop of Ghent was absent, his vicar-general sold six panels to a Brussels art dealer; the King of Prussia, Frederick William III, bought them and presented them to the Kaiser Friedrich Museum in Berlin. There they remained until 1920. Meanwhile, the Adam and Eve panels were bought by the Belgian Government and placed in the Musée des Beaux Arts in Brussels, while copies were left in the cathedral. When World War I broke out the canon of the cathedral decided that the panels remaining in their possession should be hidden. They were wrapped up and taken on a scrap-dealer's cart to a private house, where they were stored in safety. When the Germans reached

Ghent they were given a letter from the Minister of Science and Arts stating that the panels were in Britain. This they refused to believe. They interrogated the bishop, but as he had not been told what had happened he maintained in all innocence that he did not know where they were – they had disappeared during his absence. He had to sign a letter confirming that the Germans had not taken them. The Germans never realized that the panels had been hidden in an interrogation room of a nearby house that they had commandeered.

Soon after World War I, in accordance with the Treaty of Versailles, Germany had to return the panels in the Kaiser Friedrich Museum to Ghent. When I went there I heard the last chapter in the story. In the 1930s the cathedral was burgled and one panel was taken away. A few days later the Bishop of Ghent received a ransom demand for 2 million Belgian francs. He refused to pay. The police succeeded in tracing the thief, who turned out to be a respectable local businessman. He was arrested and taken to police headquarters for questioning, but while he was there he suffered a heart attack and died without having revealed the hiding-place of the stolen panel. His house was searched from top to bottom and his garden was dug up, but without success, and to this day the panel has not been found. Subsequently a replica was made for the cathedral.

Because the six panels from the Berlin museum had been re-turned to Ghent, Hitler decided when he occupied Belgium that he wanted the whole altar-piece. Count Wolff Metternich told me that when he heard that the director of the Bavarian State Gallery had arrived in Paris on a special mission, he realized something was afoot. Then he heard from one of his contacts that Hitler wanted the altar-piece for Linz. At first the Vichy govern-ment, acting for the Belgians, refused to surrender it. But Hitler's emissary was not to be deterred. Laval was contacted, and he readily agreed to its removal. The emissary from Munich wasted no time but went straight to Pau with suitable transportation. The altar-piece was removed under armed guard and taken in great secrecy to Germany. Wolff Metternich and his assistants had tried to intervene but without success.

Nevertheless Hitler never removed any works of art from French museums. This was not because of any love he had for the French, Count Wolff Metternich explained to me, but for a quite different reason. He had decided that France's greatest art treasures were to be written into the peace negotiations as part of France's compensation to Germany. Meanwhile he could wait and let the works of art be well cared for in their rural hiding-places. But objects of German origin – as for instance those in the Musée de l'Armée, mentioned earlier – were to be returned to Germany.

Once the Einsatzstab Rosenberg had gained complete control over confiscation and disposal of Jewish-owned works of art and, with the approval of Hitler and Göring, flaunted the frequent protests of the Kunstschutz, Count Wolff Metternich found himself isolated. Nominally still the head of the army's official Kunstschutz, he was simply being tolerated until the time he could be dismissed. Nevertheless he was sometimes able to circumvent the ERR's activities. It had come to his knowledge that a certain valuable privately owned art collection was to be confiscated by Vichy officials under pressure from the ERR. Knowing that the owner had left it to the local museum on condition he kept it during his lifetime, Wolff Metternich privately forewarned him of the impending confiscation. The owner was thus able to hand it over to the museum officials, who stored it away in a safe deposit.

Count Wolff Metternich had also made a secret arrangement with the French Government art authorities whereby he would give them detailed lists of all works of art sent to Germany by the ERR. Thanks to his efforts, the restitution commission of the French Government was able to return nearly all the confiscated items to their rightful owners after the war. For this clandestine work General de Gaulle later awarded him the Legion of Honour. Meanwhile his days in Paris were numbered. Göring was incensed that the Kunstschutz had tried to interfere in his activities, and reported him to Hitler. Soon afterwards the High Command relieved him of his job, which was taken over by his assistant, von Tischowitz, who also – though without much success – did what he could to oppose the ERR.

Count Wolff Metternich returned now to his old job as curator of the Rhineland museums. He was not persecuted either in his private life or his work, though he had expected to be. He believed this was because he had considerable inside knowledge about the ERR and about Göring's activities, as well as having influential friends in the German High Command. Hitler no doubt did not want to stir things up, and realized that Wolff Metternich knew all about the Reichsmarschall's acquisitions on his frequent visits to Paris. According to ERR records Göring 'purchased' 700 works of art at the auctions of confiscated items, among them Chardin's *Joyeuse de Volant*, Fragonard's *Young Girl with Chinese Figure*, four nudes by Cranach the Elder and the Younger, a Boucher *Venus*, Teniers's *Adam and Eve in Paradise*, not to mention tapestries from Beauvais and even Cardinal Mazarin's writing-desk. Nor would Hitler have wanted it known that the projected Linz gallery was being supplied with loot partly from Jewish collections. Such was the story that Wolff Metternich told me in 1964, since when, after many years of active work at the Herziana Library in Rome, he has died.

When I was in Paris in 1964 I was told that a Madame Rose Valland had been deeply involved in clandestine work inside the ERR records office. Though she was reluctant at first to talk about her wartime exploits I was at length able to interview her. Before the war, she told me, she had worked as an art historian in the administration of the Louvre. When the Einsatzstab Rosenberg established their collecting-point for confiscated works at the Jeu de Paume in 1940, she realized what was happening and decided to infiltrate the organization. With her knowledge of the arts she had no difficulty in being taken on as a clerk in the inventory department. The work, carried out under German supervision, consisted of carefully filing detailed information about all works of art passing through the hands of the ERR – former ownership, how and when confiscated, value and history of the object, and a photograph. On dispatch to Germany, the recipient and buyer of the object were also noted down. After consultation with her former colleagues she decided to make a duplicate copy of all the information filed. Working laboriously and for long hours, she succeeded in her task without ever being detected, and the information she obtained proved to be invaluable after the war for establishing ownership.

Madame Valland's greatest *coup* was the saving of many of the Louvre treasures. When the Allies were advancing towards Paris in 1944 the ERR was ordered to leave the city, but they wanted to take all they could with them. Madame Valland discovered that Colonel von Behr, its chief, was listing a selection of the most valuable objects still in the Louvre for immediate dispatch to

Germany. She took careful notes from the list of items to be taken, comprising 1,200 paintings from the art section. One hundred and forty-eight of these, with other loot from the Louvre, had been loaded into Luftwaffe trucks, she discovered, which were driving off in convoy to the Gare de l'Est. She immediately contacted the railway workers' chief, who was also in the Resistance, telling him what had happened and asking him to mark the crates carefully with code numbers, and to find out the train's destination. A couple of hours later her telephone rang at the office. 'Abbeville,' said a voice. Now that she knew the train's destination, she rang another section of the Resistance and told them what was in the crates. Everything possible must be done to delay the train, she said, even if the tracks had to be torn up. 'Keep the train near Paris' was her final instruction.

Meanwhile Colonel von Behr and his team, under military escort, were supervising the loading of the crates on to the train. It was time for it to leave; but the crew were in no hurry. Slowly they started to take it to Le Bourget, on the outskirts of Paris. But some of the tracks had been taken up, and by the time they were repaired forty-eight hours had passed. Colonel von Behr was getting impatient. The train moved off again but was re-routed because of further reported damage to the track near Aulnay. Then suddenly the air-brakes failed to operate; slowly the train returned to Paris for repairs. One hold-up succeeded another: the engine broke down, tracks were taken up, and after twenty-eight days the train was still held up.

During all this time the Allies were advancing on Paris, which was being evacuated by the Germans and had been declared an open city, chiefly because the commander-in-chief refused to destroy it by making a last stand as Hitler had intended. Madame Valland, anxiously waiting for the Allies to arrive, was trying to think of further ways of delaying the train. The Allied forces had reached Rambouillet, near Paris, but could get no farther for three days. The French Resistance fighters were harassing the retreating Germans. Von Behr was getting desperate in his determination to get the Louvre treasures to Germany. In a final effort to do so he had all the railwaymen his forces could muster brought to the train, threatening them that unless they shifted it forthwith his men would open fire on them. He commandeered a brand-new engine, and put guards on all the trucks and with the driver. He personally inspected the train and then gave the order for departure.

He nearly got away with it. But the railyards the train had to run through had already been taken by General Leclerc's French Armoured Division; the train with its precious cargo was safe. In the mêlée that followed Colonel von Behr made his escape to Germany, where later on he and his wife committed suicide. They did so in style on von Behr's estate, drinking a farewell toast in poisoned vintage champagne.

Belgium did not suffer as France did. In Belgium the Kunstschutz carefully protected both historic buildings and museums. Moreover, workers and materials were even provided to repair damage suffered during hostilities. It was only when the Germans were in retreat that looting and wanton destruction occurred, and this was mainly carried out by Hitler's own tough and revengeful Waffen SS – elite troops who fought a fanatical rearguard action, willing to die for the glory of the Führer. For their commanders military considerations came first. In Hoogstraeten the SS commander deliberately had the historic and architecturally beautiful church tower dynamited, his justification being that it was a potential observation post for the advancing Allied armies. Besides, he declared, an ancient building was as useless as an old man, and the survival of strong men like himself was more important.

Property was taken from churches in Bruges before the Allies reached it. Michelangelo's famous sculpture of the Madonna and Child from the Church of Notre Dame in Bruges was kept in a specially constructed shelter in the north aisle, but just before the Allied troops arrived, a German officer with naval personnel drove up in a truck and removed the statue regardless of the churchwardens' protests. The triptych *Adoration of the Shepherds* by Pourbus, a sixteenth-century Flemish painter who lived and worked in Bruges, was also taken, though for some reason two panels with the donors' portraits were left, as well as fifteen other valuable paintings, among them a Caravaggio, a Van Dyck, and an Isenbrandt.

This looting was explained away by Goebbels in a broadcast shortly afterwards. The art treasures had been removed, he said, to save them from destruction or transportation from Europe to a country alien to the spirit and environment of Bruges. The Bishop of Bruges received a letter informing him that the removal had been at the request of the commander-in-chief. And Bruges was not the only town to suffer. The Church of St Pierre in Louvain had two panels representing the Last Supper and two of the martyrdom of St Erasmus taken. These were not recovered from Germany until 1946.

Belgium suffered the loss of many of her church bells. Every church in Belgium was restricted to the use of one bell. When German soldiers came to take the bells away from the fifteenth-century Church of St Michel in Ghent, they found the priest and parishioners in the midst of tolling them. The soldiers had to threaten armed force to achieve the surrender of the bells. After this incident the following words appeared on the wall of the church tower: 'Here we have just the rope left with which to hang yourself.'

Like Belgium, the little Duchy of Luxembourg did not suffer much from direct confiscations, in spite of being a German-speaking country. An historic collection of arms was taken, but en route to Germany some courageous Luxembourgers seized part of the collection and dispersed it among different museums. The conservateur of the Musée Historique successfully opposed confiscations, and as long as the Kunstschutz art commission was in control the museums were carefully protected. But in Asembourg and Colmar châteaux were occupied and vandalized by groups of Hitler Youth from Germany, and the Benedictine Abbey of St Maurice was turned into a Hitler school.

The Nazi authorities decided in 1944 that Luxembourg's famous Pescatore collection of paintings must be 'safeguarded' from Allied air raids by removal to a bunker near Esternach on the frontier with Germany. The curator insisted on inspecting the depository, and reported to the Germans that it was so damp that all the pictures would suffer damage. Before the Germans had time to think up a reply he secretly removed the collection to his own museum, which unknown to the authorities had become a storage-house for treasures. There the conservateur had hidden the archives of the Luxembourg Chambre des Députés, with other documents and books that the Germans were seeking. Everything was packed in wooden crates and labelled 'Historic Collections'. By this simple ruse valuable records were saved from destruction, especially necessary since Goebbels had banned many of the books.

As the combined Allied armies landed in Italy and France, SHAEF Headquarters, under General Eisenhower's command, issued a directive to all troops that, consistent with military necessities, all damage to structures, objects, or documents of cultural, artistic, archaeological or historical value was to be avoided. All commanding generals were ordered to ensure prevention of looting, wanton damage and sacrilege by their troops. To implement this order groups of MFA&A (Monuments, Fine Arts & Archaeology) officers from Britain and the United States, all of them art historians, museum curators or archaeologists in civilian life, moved in as soon as a town had been taken. Their job was to assess any damage to historic buildings, organize the protection of art treasures, place certain areas out of bounds to troops, and later on to search for works of art looted by the Nazis.

In France, it was not until the Allied Fine Arts Commission reached Paris after the Liberation that the extent of the art confiscations was appreciated. The disappearance from Pau of the Van Eyck altar-piece became a priority concern; all the ERR members who knew anything about it had long since left. The existence of the Linz project only became known at this time, and its scope, according to Lt-Colonel Professor Webb, made the MFA&A officers realize what an immense task lay ahead of them. Professor Webb was amazed to discover how well the French museum authorities had, with one or two exceptions, distributed their works of art all over the country and out of reach of the Nazis, a policy that had been planned before the outbreak of hostilities. He recalled, for instance, some very valuable medieval glass that he had expected to find destroyed but which was found intact in Normandy. It had been stored in various insignificant locations. It was not until the Allies actually crossed the frontiers of Nazi Germany that they came to realize something of the chaos Hitler had brought about in the art world.

After twenty days of brave resistance against the German invaders in the spring of 1940 the Dutch armed forces were obliged to surrender against overwhelming odds. The ruthless aerial blitz on Rotterdam, which destroyed the city, had put an end to further hostilities. In anticipation of an attack of this kind, being aware of the Nazi methods employed in Poland, the Dutch museum authorities had taken their own precautions. All valuable art treasures had been evacuated from the Rijksmuseum in

Amsterdam and the Mauritshus in The Hague to specially constructed underground bunkers in the dunes of northern Holland. However, apart from the initial devastation of Rotterdam the Germans carried out their occupation of the Netherlands as smoothly as possible. The splendours of Amsterdam had always impressed them, and in any event they did not want to stir up unnecessary resistance among the population. The Kunstschutz saw to it that none of the exhibits in Dutch museums or works of art stored in museum depositories were touched.

The Reich commissioner for the Netherlands was the Austrian Seyss-Inquart who, although he had been under oath to the Austrian chancellor Schuschnigg, had in 1938 drafted Hitler's ultimatum to Schuschnigg which was to terminate the independence of Austria. Seyss-Inquart was responsible directly to Hitler. His first act on coming to power in the Netherlands was to issue an order contravening article 46 of the Hague Convention. All property of people accused of 'promoting activities hostile to the Third Reich will be confiscated'. Although the order was aimed mainly at Jews, the Dutch Royal family was not excluded from it. Their treasures were confiscated too, after Queen Wilhelmina and her government had gone into exile in Britain before the arrival in the Netherlands of the Germans. Having issued his new order Seyss-Inquart wasted no time in calling in his old Austrian crony, Dr Katjetan Mühlmann, who had been in charge of the ruthless confiscations of Polish art treasures. In Holland, however, he had to tread more carefully.

The newly created 'Dienststelle Mühlmann' (Mühlmann Department), apart from 'safeguarding' and confiscating Jewish-owned art treasures, also became the purchasing office for the Linz museum project. Hitler's art expert and buyer for Linz at that time, Dr Hans Posse, wasted no time in coming to The Hague to purchase confiscated works of art at auctions as well as to buy directly from Dutch art dealers and private collectors. By the time he arrived the art market prices had already sky-rocketed. Under the German occupation a roaring trade in works of art had developed. Dr Posse was obliged to appoint middlemen to compete in the art purchases.

The Dienststelle Mühlmann proved to be of great value to the Linz project. Through its activities, within a year Dr Posse acquired eighty valuable paintings for Linz. Among these were two portraits by Rubens, Canaletto's *View of San Marco*, a self-portrait by Rembrandt, and many other works by Dutch and Flemish artists of the seventeenth century.

To ingratiate himself with the Führer, Mühlmann presented him with an album containing photographs of most of the purchases. He could not of course have foreseen that this present from 'a loyal servant to the Führer' would be the means of exposing him, for the album was found eventually by the Allied fine arts teams in Hitler's private library. When Mühlmann claimed that his organization was merely a legal purchasing department, he was confronted with the picture album. Not only did it contain photographs of some confiscated paintings but the names of the Jewish owners besides. Mühlmann could not explain away this incriminating pictorial evidence.

Reichsmarschall Göring already had the pick of works of art confiscated in France, and he now appointed his own agent in Holland. But to his chagrin Dr Posse had a greater pull in Holland, acting as he was on behalf of the Führer, and Posse took great pleasure in outbidding the Reichsmarschall.

The acquisitions for the Linz museum by Dr Posse were considerable. Had the project materialized it would have contained a collection of some of the best Dutch and Flemish masters. Göring was a great admirer of such paintings. He had set his heart on acquiring a Vermeer, and accordingly he instructed his agent to obtain one, cost what it may. Eventually a painting attributed to Vermeer was offered him and, after expert advice and much haggling, he purchased the picture, *Christ and the Woman Taken in Adultery*, for the tidy sum of 1,600,000 guilders. He had been obliged to sell a number of paintings from his own Karinhall collection to pay out this large sum of money, and the work became one of his proudest possessions. Although Dutch and other art experts believed it to be a genuine Vermeer, after the war they all were proved to have been hoaxed.

CHAPTER NINE

Art under Fire

With the German Army's victories in Poland and the West, Hitler's artistic ambition to be the great architect of his country took on new dimensions. Despite military operations and the construction of defences along the Channel coast against the Allies, the Führer continued to be preoccupied with the Linz project. Albert Speer was concentrating all his attention on defensive work, of which he was in charge, which meant that additional architects had to be assigned to the project. Eventually Professor Hermann Giesler was appointed by Hitler. Giesler had been developing the Führer's plans for a modernized Munich, birthplace of the Nazi Party and known as the capital of the *Bewegung* (the Movement). The Party headquarters was there in the Braune Haus, a villa it had acquired in its early days and converted into offices, and still the symbol of its early struggles. A new headquarters was planned, and next to it a domed tomb destined for Hitler's remains. Hitler's grandiose idea was to create five so-called 'Reichs' cities. For Berlin, as capital, Speer had already produced detailed models and actually built parts of them. Nuremberg, with its gigantic and impressive stadium, was the city of the Party rallies. Then there was Hamburg, the great Hansa city, and Munich, destined to be a place of pilgrimage where future generations could pay homage to the Führer's tomb. The last, Linz, would be the centre of the art world. Hitler had always admired Budapest, with its ancient buildings on both sides of the Danube, and had decided Linz was to become the German version of that beautiful city.

Giesler was a young and talented architect who, according to Speer, understood Hitler's ideas and knew how to implement his detailed plans and sketches. Notwithstanding all the military problems facing him and the disasters that were to come, Hitler would keep in touch week by week with the progress of his plans, visiting Giesler personally in his Munich studio or calling him to the Berghof to discuss new ideas. He always listened attentively to Giesler and showed no signs of temperament. The planning became his life's hobby, absorbing him right up until his final days in the Berlin bunker.

While Dr Posse, through dealers and ERR confiscations, was accumulating a vast selection of treasures for the Linz art centre, the actual building programme in Linz seems to have got off to a slow start. Hitler did not give the order to commence work until 1940. The total plan was an ambitious one, as Speer has described it. There was to be a large Gauhaus, or district headquarters, for the Party, with a hall accommodating 35,000 people. The building was to be surmounted by a bell tower, and below it would be a crypt and Hitler's tomb. On the latter detail Speer must have been incorrect, however, as Hitler's tomb was planned for Munich. There was also to be a special tower above a small tomb for the remains of Hitler's parents, which were to be transferred from Leonding cemetery to this last resting-place. A Glockenspiel would play music by Bruckner several times a day in memory of the great German composer and son of Linz.

The banks of the Danube were to have a series of impressive buildings: a town hall, a large theatre, military headquarters, and a monument commemorating the annexation of Austria in 1938. I was told by another source that a monument to Bismarck was planned for the Urfahr Danube site where Hitler had lived as a boy. According to Hitler, the people of Linz had always considered the Prussian statesman as their symbol of German power. This contention must have been virtually baseless, however, since only a few extreme German nationalists would have so regarded him, the Prussians never being popular in Austria at any time, even under Nazi rule. In addition, there was to be a technical high school and a large modern hotel, both on the banks of the Danube with a view across the river to the beautiful wooded hills that surround the town. The concert hall and Bruckner Centre were to be devoted to the composer, as Bayreuth is to Wagner. There was to be a library of 250,000 books, some of them from Hitler's own collection, with his special bookmark on the inside cover. A cinema was to be built for film premières. Hitler was a great film fan and would often have films shown at the Berghaus, even those banned to German audiences. Restaurants and parks, a theatre and opera-house, for which Hitler had already chosen an orchestra, and a special hall for variety shows completed the plan. If all this had materialized, it would certainly have been impressive to say the least. Linz would have become a combination of the old town integrated if not harmonizing with the Nazi-inspired architecture of the new Germanic 'culture'. Speer was to build the art gallery and the stadium overlooking the city. Nearby was to be Hitler's retirement house, designed by Giesler, consisting of a square building with four turrets looking down over the city from the heights of the Freinberg.

The first job tackled in Linz was the Nibelungen Brücke, or Bridge of the Nibelungs, spanning the fast-flowing Danube. This massive suspension bridge was to replace the old one connecting Linz proper with the suburb of Urfahr, which as a boy Hitler must have crossed daily to the suburban home where he lived with his mother. The new plans demanded the raising of the level of the bridge, and this meant demolishing a few old houses to widen the approach. There were to be monumental statues at each end of the bridge, and Graf Plettenburg, the well-known German sculptor famous for his oversized statues of virile men and well-proportioned women, was commissioned to create four characters from the Nibelung Saga, including Siegfried and Kriemhild.

By 1943 considerable progress had been made on the building of the bridge and Hitler took time off from his wartime headquarters to visit his home town. Albert Speer describes Hitler's reactions to the plaster models of the statues that had been placed at the southern end of the bridge for his inspection. He commented on Siegfried's fabulous stance and the way his hands clasped his sword, and remarked that the half-naked Kriemhild was more erotic than many a work of art. (Some wit suggested that her bosom would provide a good roosting-place for pigeons.) He decided that when the four statues were finished they would form the nucleus of the new Linz. But they were never completed, and today the modern bridge is the only reminder of Hitler's grand design for the city.

Meanwhile Hitler was leaving nothing to chance in the organization of the new art gallery. Various experts had been appointed: Posse in charge of paintings; Dr Dworschak from the Vienna Kunsthistorisches Museum responsible for coins; a Dr Rupprecht for armoury; and a certain Wollfhardt for the specially planned library. As the art treasures poured in ever greater numbers into the Führerbau depository in Munich for Hitler's personal selection, it seemed that a second museum might be needed in Linz to house them all. The ERR sent large leather-bound catalogues of confiscated treasures from which Hitler could choose objects with which to stock his favourite German museums, and in particular to fortify the Linz project.

It must not be forgotten that the entire Linz project, the ERR operation, and the distribution of lists of confiscated objects were kept a close secret. Apart from Hitler, his immediate associates, and the art experts actually involved in the operation, nobody knew of it – though many art dealers must have guessed something of what was afoot. However, they were concerned only with the business side of it and avoided asking questions. Even Hitler's close photographer friend Heinrich Hoffmann was not allowed to breathe a word about it. The exact details were known only to Posse and his successor Dr Voss, who were responsible for the acquisition of works of art.

Until the finalization of his Linz project and the appointment of Posse, Hitler bought only pictures, for cash, for his own small private collection. He and Heinrich Hoffmann had similar tastes in art: Hoffmann would acquire pictures for Hitler through Frau Dietrich's Gallery in Munich (Frau Dietrich's daughter was a friend of Hitler's mistress, Eva Braun). Hitler admired the Italian Renaissance, and the Baroque period; in his Berghof at Obersalzburg he hung a favourite Baroque painting, a nude by Bordone which he had bought from Haberstock. He disliked skinny figure paintings such as Cranach's and preferred more buxom nudes. His agents were instructed to buy up nineteenth-century painters such as Overbeck, Hans von Marees, Moritz von Schwind, Piloty and many others, including his favourite Hans Makart. As mentioned earlier, he seems to have been obsessed with Grützner in particular. He liked clear detail in paintings, such as he had striven for in his own pedantic watercolours. All these painters were now to be fully represented in the Linz gallery, which would become a monument to 'safe' art for the new Germany and from which non-German artists after the eighteenth century would of necessity be excluded.

Although Hitler's Special Mission Linz had priority over the other Nazi leaders' art collections, it was inevitable that rivalry should develop over the acquisition of the spoils. Bormann had immense power over the disposal of confiscated works of art, but he was not a serious collector. It was Göring who collected art in the grand style, especially priding himself on his collection at Karinhall, which he had begun long before Hitler planned his private collection of mediocre nineteenth-century German artists. Göring had been at it ever since his service as a fighter pilot in World War I. But it was only after Hitler came to power in 1933 that he conceived the idea of creating his own museum of European art that could be left to the nation. Karinhall and Berlin were both possible locations for it. If it had been the former it would have been turned into a tourists' Mecca, with a direct railway link from Berlin.

It was Hitler's idea to create a 'finders-keepers' agreement, the funds to be provided by the State. This was what gave Göring the impetus to embark upon large-scale collecting, from architectural fragments to Old Masters to modern paintings, tapestries, carpets and jewellery. Göring appreciated his acquisitions and would spend time seriously studying a masterpiece, but he took professional advice rather than relying entirely on his own taste. His first adviser was the art historian and dealer Binder from Berlin, but he was soon succeeded by Walter Andreas Hofer, a comparatively small Berlin dealer who also had contacts in Switzerland.

Hofer's first contact with Göring came about when he sold him a painting in 1937. He then became not only adviser to Göring but official buyer for Karinhall. It was agreed that he should remain an independent dealer in Berlin and work for Göring on a commission basis, with the proviso that he could keep anything

Göring rejected for his own business. When Göring appointed Hofer curator of Karinhall he wanted to pay him a salary, but Hofer refused point-blank. He was well aware of the advantages he had over rival dealers: not only had he the protection and support of one of the most powerful men in the Reich, but all doors were open to him wherever he went in search of works of art. He was able also on many occasions to give protection to Jews who could offer him a coveted picture in exchange, or with whom he had had past dealings. For his part Göring knew that Hofer would not cheat him. If a picture was too expensive for Göring, back it would go, according to the terms of the agreement. Hofer was most unpopular with the other German dealers and the middlemen in occupied countries who wanted to sell direct to Göring. His business trips were always carefully planned with Göring's backing, and he would bargain for rock-bottom prices. Even the ERR could not stop him from getting hold of nineteenth-century pictures, which he then sold for high prices on the Berlin art market. Göring's habit of 'purchasing' confiscated French collections was Hofer's idea.

There is no doubt whatever that the flair and taste embodied in Göring's collection at Karinhall would have made the Linz collection look second-rate. In a letter to Rosenberg about his acquisition of pictures confiscated by the ERR, Göring congratulated himself in 1940 on owning probably the most important private art collection in Germany, if not in Europe. Karinhall – the country house in East Prussia he had built and named after his first wife, long dead – contained early German masters, Dürers, Cranachs, Dutch and Flemish paintings including some especially valuable seventeenth-century ones, a small selection of French eighteenth-century works, some valuable Italian masterpieces, some French Gothic art, and some of the finest Impressionists. After the war Göring's family claimed back the pictures he had bought early on with his own money.

On two occasions Göring arranged for prominent Jewish art dealers, who had supplied him with pictures he wanted, to escape to Switzerland, and even to take their money with them. This was done on Hofer's initiative, as they provided useful neutral contacts for further deals. If it was in his own interest, Göring would be indifferent as to whether a dealer was Jewish or not. Nor would he put pressure on anyone to sell a work of art he wanted – any 'persuasion', with suggestions of dire consequences in the case of refusal, he left to others to carry out on his behalf. He liked to see himself as a Renaissance man, dedicated to the arts, and wanted all his deals to appear to be above board.

Göring established a so-called *Kunstfond*, or art fund, headed by General Karl Bodenschatz. Its assets were always between one and two million Reichsmarks, out of which he paid for his art acquisitions. Profits from his own deals – selling off his unwanted paintings to Nazi gauleiters at inflated prices – went into the fund. The buyers did not mind paying a high price, since they could boast that their purchases came from Göring's own collection at Karinhall. Göring realized this only too well, and encouraged such sales; he often bragged about the profits he had made. Into the Kunstfond flowed contributions from big business concerns and war contractors to the Luftwaffe who were dependent on the Reichsmarschall's goodwill.

Some contributions would be in kind. On his birthday in 1942 the city of Berlin presented Göring with a Tintoretto taken from a German museum and valued at over 200,000 marks. This greatly annoyed Goebbels, who had been trying to channel all available resources towards the war effort, and from then on presentations made to Göring were much less valuable. Collecting Gobelin tapestries was another of Göring's special interests and he loved to hang them on the walls of Karinhall. Many came from confiscation sales in France. When Hitler annexed Austria, Göring was very quick off the mark and 'borrowed' Gobelins from the State collection in Vienna. These were never returned, and it seems that they ended up in East Germany.

Hitler and Göring pursued their rival quests for art treasures to the bitter end. Even during the most critical days of the war both would find time to inspect and select objects for their respective projects. Anything confiscated or 'legally' acquired by Göring or other Nazi officials had to be photographed, and a copy of the photograph sent to the Führer. Should the Führer later want one of these items for Linz he could refer to the photograph and requisition it. It was Bormann who had suggested this procedure to Hitler, who immediately passed the order to Göring. As a result massive albums with detailed information of confiscated art were kept, which made the post-war restitution work of the Allied art commissions that much easier.

Behind all the activities concerned with works of art lingered the figure of Bormann, Hitler's shadow, his unobtrusive and trusted secretary, feared for his ruthlessness by many. He was never far from his leader; he even carried scraps of paper in his pocket for Hitler to doodle on when he was telephoning. It was he who gave the orders regarding the disposition of confiscated art; he edged Hoffmann away from his position as Hitler's art adviser, and he had little time for Ribbentrop. And it was Bormann too who instigated – with Hitler's approval – the confiscation of Church property throughout Germany and Austria. Ecclesiastical art treasures, altar-pieces and libraries of ancient manuscripts were seized, monastries were dissolved and monks forced to go back into the world. In Austria, the famous Abbeys of Kremsmünster, Göttweig and St Florian, among others, suffered this fate. St Florian and its church had been much admired by Hitler in his youth when he visited it, but this did not stop its closure. The famous Vienna Boys' College of the Benedictine order of the Schottengymnasium was also closed, and the teaching staff of priests expelled. Some of the expropriated abbeys – Kremsmünster, and Buxheim in Bavaria, for instance – were used for storing some of Hitler's looted art. Others were used as holiday and training centres for the Hitler Youth, as at Asembourg and Colmar in Luxembourg. The grim facts about Hitler's persecution of all the various religious denominations are now widely known. Without exception he regarded them as enemies of the State, out of step with Nazi education and the philosophy of Rosenberg.

In 1941 Hitler created a new propaganda unit, the combat artists. He issued an order to the commander-in-chief of the armed forces to find suitable painters, and these artists were sent to Potsdam to be taught by Luitpold Adam, a war artist from World War I. They were then dispatched to the front in uniform for three months to make sketches, after which they went back to Potsdam to turn them into finished pictures. By 1942 eighty artists were working in this way; they even formed their own special units, such as the Waffen SS Kurt Eggers group. They worked within the navy and the air force as well as the army.

These combat artists were ordered to make their work detailed and realistic. Research institutes were instructed to experiment with different painting materials, and historical investigations of painting techniques were carried out. The pictures, most of which ended up in American archives after the war, were pure propaganda for the Party and in particular for the Waffen SS forces. War was represented heroically: as with all German official newsreels, no German dead were to be seen, only those of the enemy. However, Germans were permitted to be seen as wounded, or as absent heroes mourned by comrades. The enemy, on the other hand, was shown as completely devastated.

The Munich exhibition of German art was opened by Hitler in person every year, and he expressed his opinion in no uncertain terms if the exhibits did not come up to his expectations. He was shown the pictures for submission to the Venice Biennale, which in 1942 were very poor. Unbelievable daubs, he commented, reminding him of the 'degenerate' art he had banned. Art exhibitions were encouraged in the Reich and a considerable amount of prize-money was made available for artists. Many a mediocre artist could make a good living churning out genre paintings of German country life or patriotic subjects. One painter specialized in heroic war scenes for postcards and made a fortune from sales to the forces. Apart from the combat artists, artists were exempt from conscription into the forces.

In 1943 in Vienna an exhibition called 'Young Art' was planned by Baldur von Schirach. Von Schirach had replaced Bürckel as Gauleiter, and as an educated and aristocratic man was more popular with the Viennese than the brusque, Germanic Bürckel. Apart from two busts, one of Hitler and one of Mussolini, the exhibits were not at all along the prescribed Nazi lines. Unfortunately the opening day coincided with the German surrender at Stalingrad, and at the last moment the much-heralded official opening at the Künstlerhaus had to be cancelled. The exhibition opened, nevertheless, but lasted only a week. Hitler was furious with von Schirach, who told Albert Speer after the war in Spandau Prison that from then onwards Hitler ignored any artistic advice volunteered by him.

CHAPTER TEN

Italy's Art Rescued

As early as 1939 Hitler and Mussolini had signed a treaty in which it was stated that all works of art of German authorship or origin were to be returned by the State of Italy to Germany. This referred mainly to the South Tyrol, which was part of the Austro-Hungarian Empire until the end of World War I and in which were held religious works of art such as medieval altar-pieces carved by German craftsmen. The treaty, however, was never honoured by Italy.

When it came to the looting of art treasures during World War II, Hitler and Göring could not proceed in Italy in the way they had in the occupied countries. Germany and Italy were Axis partners, and everything had to be above board, which meant that Italian art treasures had to be bought in the open market from established dealers. Accordingly, official buyers were appointed by Dr Posse to be responsible for works for the Linz project. Prince Philip of Hesse had the right background for the job: related to both Queen Victoria and King Frederick IV of Prussia, he had studied at Oxford, was married to one of the King of Italy's daughters, and had settled in Rome as an architect. Posse appointed him to supervise the work.

Göring, not to be outdone, used the Luftwaffe administrative headquarters in Rome as an intermediary to pay for his purchases. From receipts discovered after the war it appears that Göring spent about 18 million lire on paintings in Italy. To get them out of the country without an export permit he would make use of the German diplomatic bag. By 1942 the massive buying of art treasures for Linz and for Göring's collection forced the Italian Minister of Education, Bottai, to pass a law prohibiting the export of works of art from Italy, and as a result the purchases diminished to a mere trickle. But Göring was not easily thwarted. When he bought Memling's *Portrait of a Man* he got his agent Hofer to approach the Duce directly for a permit.

After the Allies had landed on Italian soil the attitude of the Nazis towards the Italians as well as to their art treasures changed. Though the Italians were still their allies, the Germans had little respect for their fighting qualities and, as Field-Marshal Alexander's forces advanced, the Waffen SS did not spare the Italians' feelings for their national heritage. The German High Command in Italy realized they needed their own Kunstschutz for Italy. This was duly established in Rome, at first under Wehrmacht control and then under the direction of SS Colonel Langsdorff, appointed by Himmler. Langsdorff, an art historian and professor who had been in charge of the Prussian State museums, was accountable only to Himmler and his deputy, General Wolff of the SS, and Chief of the German Security Police in Italy. Once again, Hitler must have had the Linz project in mind, and the Kunstschutz under Colonel Langsdorff began taking steps to 'protect' Italian art treasures. Among the first of these was the Italian monarchical treasure from the royal palace in Cuneo, which included King Victor Emmanuel III's precious collection of 50,000 antique gold coins dating back to the Roman Empire. The Abyssinian crown, which Mussolini had looted during his invasion of Abyssinia in 1936, was removed. The Germans' excuse was that the Allied forces' landings and their progress towards Rome imperilled their safety.

At about the same time as the German Army created their own Kunstschutz in November 1943, the War Office in London appointed the noted archaeologist, Sir Leonard Wooley, as their monuments and arts adviser with the rank of lieutenant-colonel. Not until 1944 did the Anglo-American joint Monuments, Fine

Arts and Archives group become part of the Allied armies liberating occupied Europe. Two weeks after the Allied landing in Sicily officers of the MFA&A moved in to assess the damage caused to historical monuments and works of art during the fighting, museums and art galleries having now been put out of bounds to troops. It was only when they reached Naples that they realized what the retreating Nazi units under SS command were capable of destroying. The Royal Society Library with its priceless contents had been drenched in petrol and set alight. Italian guards resisting this vandalism had been shot. From the National Library 800 cases of valuable books had been taken. The Villa Montezone at Livardi, near Nola, where the Naples State Archives had been evacuated, had been deliberately fired. Many valuable archives had been wantonly destroyed: records of the Hohenstaufen, the German princely family; the Angevin; the kings of Naples; the kings of the House of Aragon; as well as Spanish and Austrian envoy reports and records of the Bourbon dynasty covering the period 1239–1811. About seventy paintings were lost, among them the *Madonna and Child* by Luini, and an early painting by Botticelli. At Nenni, Roman galleys had been burned to ashes, and the Palazzo Ruspoli sacked by departing German troops. Sir Leonard Wooley reported many other acts of destruction. While all this was happening the Nazis were broadcasting to the Italians and to their own people that the Jews and thieves of the Allied arts commissions were looting Italian treasures. A ship had left from Sicily, they said, loaded with works of art for the British Museum and private collections.

In Naples the museum authorities had evacuated most of the valuable contents of the city's National Museum to the Benedictine monastery of Monte Cassino. With Alexander's armies approaching Monte Cassino, the German Kunstschutz and the Fascist authorities in Rome agreed that the collection should be moved. After much discussion it was taken in January 1944 to the museum of the Vatican, which was neutral. On arrival, however, the Vatican museum authorities discovered a number of items missing: two pictures by Titian, one by Claude Lorrain, a Raphael, a Tiepolo, a Palma Vecchio, as well as two cases of Roman gold objects from Pompeii and Herculaneum, a suit of armour worn by the Emperor Charles V, and five bronze statues. Evidently all these treasures had been removed in transit by the convoy's commanding officer and his men. Later it transpired that they had been carefully packed up and dispatched to Göring at Karinhall as a presentation – much to the Reichsmarschall's embarrassment – from his Hermann Göring Regiment. Göring was not prepared to get involved with outright looting. He undoubtedly admired the paintings, but had them transferred to Hitler's depository in Munich. They were eventually recovered from the depository in the Alt Aussee salt-mines.

Monte Cassino was obliterated in battle and many historic churches and monuments were destroyed in the Allied advance on Rome, which meanwhile had been declared an open city. After liberating Rome the Allies advanced on Florence, where priceless works of art, collected in depositories, were now in grave danger. The Allied art commission knew that the Italians had formed an organization behind the German lines to protect their art treasures, and the Allies were told where these treasures were stored, but what the Germans intended to do was anyone's guess. The anti-Fascist Badoglio government was in control of much of Italy, and the Germans now had no time at all for their Italian comrades-in-arms.

What actually happened in those turbulent days I was able gradually to piece together. After lengthy correspondence with official departments in Rome and with museum directors I learnt the background of the story from the vivid account of Dr Rodolfo Siviero, who headed the special art protection section of Florence's Uffizi Gallery on the outbreak of the war. When Mussolini's regime collapsed he realized that things would take a turn for the worse, but it was not the Allied bombardment he feared so much as looting by SS troops. He had already formed a secret organization known cryptically as SAP to protect the Italian art treasures. This was manned by artists, art historians and museum officials, and was divided into units, each in direct contact with the Italian partisans in the German-held regions. The Florence group, led by a painter called Bruno Becchi (later killed in the fighting), was secretly accommodated in the old post office next to the Uffizi on the pretext of their doing conservation work. Their first unofficial job, at the suggestion of the superintendent of the Uffizi, Giovanni Poggi, was to save from the Germans the historic stained glass in the Cathedral of Arezzo. They retrieved the glass, which had already come down under the bombardment, loaded it on to trucks while shells burst around them, and, taking the sheltered tree-lined road from Siena, got their precious cargo safely back to Florence.

Events were moving fast. In September 1943 Dr Siviero received from one of his Italian Army contacts a copy of a dispatch circulated to the German High Command in Italy. According to this Top Secret order the Italian Army's disbanded secret service was to re-form under the German SD. Former members were to be encouraged to re-enlist under German leadership, thus enabling the SD to gain information about anti-Fascist resistance groups. Here was an opportunity to infiltrate the SD. Siviero approached a former counter-espionage officer of the Italian secret service, known as SIM. How many anti-Fascist sympathizers had there been in the service, he asked? The former officer, now a colonel in the Carabinieri, was intrigued by the question and undertook to recruit retired members of SIM for the new cause. He was provided with ample funds by Siviero, who warned him he was likely to be shot if caught. The colonel merely laughed.

Two weeks later the colonel supplied Siviero with a list of the names of eighteen former SIM officers who would ostensibly re-enlist with the Germans. The SD engaged them. Siviero's organization now had its own men in the Milan, Florence and Bologna branches of the SD, and the network was expanding still further. These infiltrators had various clandestine jobs assigned to them, the foremost being to keep the Allied command informed of German military movements, and the Italian partisans of any actions planned against them by the SD. Advance warnings were to be given to those about to be taken into custody by the Gestapo and to Jews about to be deported, and plans for confiscating art treasures were to be reported. The Florence group, under Becchi's command, used the little Café Porcellino as a 'letter-box'. The barman there was one of the group and would pass on information received by word of mouth from informers who could be trusted. A 'safe house' was established in the apartment of a Professor Giorgio Castelfranco. The Gestapo never discovered this hide-out.

The first information that came through was that the Kunstschutz planned to 'acquire' for Karinhall Fra Angelico's *Annunciation*, which was in the Franciscan monastery near San

Giovanni Valdarno. Siviero's organization went into action. Two Franciscan monks in Florence, both working for the organization, visited the monastery and removed the painting. When the Kunstschutz asked for an explanation, the superintendent of the Uffizi Gallery replied that religious masterpieces came under the jurisdiction of the Vatican museum authorities, as caretakers of Church property in Italy, and that they had ordered the picture's removal.

German demands for the removal of other Italian masterpieces to the Reich caused serious rifts with the Italian authorities. The latter were able to delay matters, however. As Siviero remarked, 'the Italian administration was like an old streetcar which rattles along and frequently stops altogether'. Although the SD collaborated with the Gestapo, neither ever suspected that the leaks came from inside its own organization. The Germans never understood the Italian mentality and very few could speak the language well, so they were at a great disadvantage in dealing with the Italians.

The first real scoop for the Siviero group came when three German dispatches, documents from the Kunstschutz offices in Florence, were handed to Bruno Becchi by one of the 'insiders'. These stated that a meeting had been arranged in the German consul's home in Florence to discuss the future of Florence's art treasures. Two SD men from Germany were shortly to arrive. Orders had come through from Hitler and Himmler that the removal of art works from the nearby villas where they had been stored should be formalized. Siviero and his group knew that the art works were going to be moved, possibly even destroyed. Through secret channels the liaison officer of the Allied Mediterranean command, Captain Stanhope Wright, was alerted to the German's intentions. The two SD men arrived in Florence and moved into the Pensione Piccoli in the Via Tornabuoni. Through a lieutenant friend who frequented the *pensione* Siviero was able to get a room there, and struck up an acquaintance with an SD man who was also a well-known art historian. This individual had come to make an on-the-spot check of all the art stores in the Florence area, and with the assistance of collaborators he soon had a list of the contents of the stores in the villas at Montegufoni and Montagnana.

Siviero's group, unfortunately, did not themselves have the

means of preventing the Germans from evacuating the works of art. The Germans had even raised the question of destroying them if evacuation were impossible, a fate from which the little group had no hope of protecting them. All that Siviero's group could do was to keep a close check on the Germans' movements. Luckily the evacuation became public knowledge, because the Germans had decided to exploit its propaganda value. The German Army would protect Europe's cultural heritage from Allied vandalism, the radio announced.

Poggi, superintendent of the Uffizi, was informed by the German consul that works from the Uffizi and Pitti Galleries were not going to be moved from their depository. Some were housed in a railway tunnel at Incisa Valdarno, close to the front line. Meanwhile Bruno Becchi was keeping a close watch on the Villa Pucci Bossi storehouse at Montagnana. On the orders of Colonel Langsdorff of the Kunstschutz, the contents were to be evacuated by the 362 Division under General Greiner, stationed at Montespertoli, near several art depots.

The first convoy got under way at the beginning of July 1944. Two weeks later the remaining works of art, under the supervision of Langsdorff himself, were taken away in trucks. Eleven exceptionally large paintings, which had not been crated, were left behind. The journey north towards the border was full of hazards; Allied aircraft were flying over on sorties, and some of the trucks broke down. Eventually they arrived at Bolzano, in the South Tyrol. The Italians, who were getting worried about the fate of the transports, demanded to inspect the South Tyrol depots, but the Germans refused them permission. Meanwhile Rome radio was broadcasting reports of the theft of Italian art treasures by the Germans.

At this time a Top Secret communication addressed to Himmler came into the hands of one of Siviero's contacts. It noted that Langsdorff had carried out the Führer's order to protect Italian art treasures from Allied bombs. It mentioned the fact that there were many masterpieces in villas and castles around Florence which could not be moved for lack of transportation. Langsdorff, however, with the aid of paratroopers, had rescued under fire two famous pictures from the castle of Orvieto, namely Cranach's *Adam* and *Eve*. The Führer, it continued, had particularly admired these paintings during his visit to Florence. They had been taken to Bergamo in northern Italy; should they be sent to Hitler to dispose of? The communication, signed by General Wolff, ended by mentioning Langsdorff's removal of works of art to the South Tyrol.

This document was one of the pieces of evidence submitted by the prosecution at the Nuremberg War Crimes trial with reference to the removal of Italian works of art destined for Germany. The removal of the Cranach paintings I learnt about from another source, which mentioned six pictures hurriedly loaded by Langsdorff into a Red Cross ambulance, sandwiched between mattresses. Langsdorff had promised Poggi, of the Uffizi, a receipt for the pictures, but none was forthcoming. Instead, Poggi was sent a letter in which Langsdorff commended his work to his opposite number on the British fine arts commission, Sir Leonard Wooley.

Other secret German documents produced at the War Crimes trial showed that, earlier in 1944, despite Italian protests, the Kunstschutz had already planned to move all Florentine works of art to northern Italy. Mussolini demanded their return to Florence, but was ignored. His own government had made plans to evacuate the galleries' contents to specially prepared depots near the Italian lakes, but the Germans rejected these out of hand. By then, in any case, Mussolini was no more than a puppet of the Germans and the Axis partnership was a thing of the past.

All these activities of the Germans were being carefully monitored by Siviero's clandestine operators. In many instances the Germans played into their hands. All Top Secret written orders had to be destroyed on completion of an operation. This was done, but copies had to be sent to the German command involved in its execution, so Siviero's 'insiders' were always able to read them when they were processed through the SD.

Other clandestine operators were keeping a close watch on the movements of all convoys conveying works of art — by now transport by rail had been abandoned owing to continuous Allied air attacks. As the Germans did not use any specific army unit for the convoys but took whatever trucks and personnel were immediately available, the task of plotting the convoys' movements became extremely difficult. The Kunstschutz was anxious to keep the whole operation under cover, and by this time the Germans distrusted all Italians and did not like to be questioned. It was possible, however, to get a certain amount of information from individual soldiers, and Siviero received from one of his agents an order from Himmler to destroy all works of art that could not be removed from the depositories around Florence. On the strength of this, the Allied High Command, according to Dr Siviero, planned a last-minute parachute drop to take over the depositories. But the German order was never carried out. The Allies' rapid advance into Tuscany left the retreating German forces no time for the destruction of art stores; they were fighting for their lives against overwhelming odds.

With the Allied armies, as they fought their way northwards in Italy, went the war correspondents. Uniformed but unarmed and with their own Press Corps insignia, they were attached to the various units. Their job was to send on-the-spot accounts of the war's progress back to their newspapers and broadcasting companies. One of the most familiar voices broadcasting from the front line was that of the BBC correspondent Wynford Vaughan Thomas. In the film, *Art in Peril,* he described his unexpected discovery of priceless art treasures at Montegufoni during the battle of Florence:

> ... I had gone up into the front line. We were advancing through the wonderful Tuscan countryside just south of Florence. It looked as if we were in one of those beautiful Italian paintings – cypresses, blue sky, farmhouses. But the whole picture was suddenly changed when the Germans started firing at us. The crashing of shells makes it rather hard to appreciate the beauty of the Italian landscape!
>
> Eric Linklater was with me, and we were making for the nearest building in our jeep. It was a castle right up on the ridge. We didn't wait to see whether we were welcome or not. We rushed through a gateway into the courtyard, to find it full of Mahratta troops – Indians and some British Army signallers. We were so intent on getting shelter that we both pelted into the main hall of the castle of Sir George Sitwell. On one side we could see some superbly painted dark canvases. I stooped down and looked at them. I said to Linklater: 'They look pretty good to me but they can't be real, they must be fakes.' We went on into the hall and suddenly an Italian refugee appeared. He sank on his knees before us and exclaimed: 'Save them, save them – the masterpieces of the Uffizi gallery!' Then he dragged us both along with him and opened another door into a great hall. He

told us to wait a minute. He rushed to the nearest shuttered window and flung it open. For me it was the most dramatic moment of the whole war: as he opened the window a shaft of strong Italian sunlight shot down exactly like a spotlight on to the greatest paintings in the world.

The first one we saw was Botticelli's *Primavera*, that marvellous evocation of the Spirit of Spring painted for Lorenzo de' Medici in the middle of the fifteenth century, fragile and glowing with colour. Down came another shaft of light from the next window as it was opened. It lit up Paolo Uccello's *The Battle of San Remo*, one of the greatest perspective paintings of the world. And as the man ran down this great hall opening one window after another, shaft after shaft of light came in, and at the end of each shaft was a masterpiece.

At this moment in came Professor Cesare Fassola, the librarian of the Uffizi and a gallant man who, unknown to Wynford Vaughan Thomas and Eric Linklater, had for days been doing the rounds of the art depots on foot begging the German soldiers not to destroy Florence's art treasures. Once he found SS troops eating their meal off a valuable painting balanced on some wooden boxes. When he asked them to move the painting they laughed, and one of them deliberately stuck his knife through it. Fassola had made his way through the battle zone without any permit from the Germans, and got through to link up with the British at the Montegufoni castle belonging to Sir George Sitwell.

... We had to do what we could [continued Wynford Vaughan Thomas]. We stirred up the British colonel in charge of the fighting in that area. He wasn't too happy about us. He had a Tiger tank at the bottom of the garden firing away most of the morning. Nevertheless he stopped the engagement and put guards on the pictures. Linklater and I rushed back in our jeep to headquarters and induced the British general in command to divert the attack from the castle area. And that was how some of the greatest of Florence's works of art were saved from destruction.

The Allied forces were already approaching Radicofani and the battle for Florence was imminent. Dr Siviero managed to slip through the German lines to the Allied Intelligence Corps unit at San Casciano, where the occupation of Florence was being planned. An encircling move was first under consideration, but in the end the only solution was a frontal attack. It was a hot, dusty night when the Allied advance on Florence started. Siviero, with a British major, was in a jeep moving in a small column up the Siena road towards the outskirts of the town. But the Germans meanwhile had been mining the bridges and historic houses along the Arno and had left demolition squads in the town. Ten high explosive charges had been planted, which would have blown up most of the town, but two of Siviero's men were able to round up the forty-odd agents who were to have set them off. Nevertheless when the underground rose to fight it was not possible to save some of the world's most beautiful locations, and when Sir Leonard Wooley and his team entered Florence it was in a sorry mess. The Uffizi Gallery had been spared, but all the monuments on the north side of the Arno had been demolished. The only bridge left standing was the Ponte Vecchio – probably on Hitler's orders, for he had admired it during his State visit to Italy. The Santa Trinità Bridge had been blown up, despite being listed as a protected monument under international law, and only the supporting columns were left. A young sculptor, Gianetto Manucci, rounded up some volunteers and they dived into the Arno to recover fragments of the bridge's celebrated statues and ornamentation. A crane later raised four statues, which are now part of the modern bridge, reconstructed just like the old one from plans in the archives of the American Council of Learned Societies.

In Siena, the local partisans managed at the last minute to stop German troops taking away works of art from the depositories near the town. Success generally depended on the German officer in charge of the area. One of them, Andreas Schreiber, who had been a painter himself in civilian life, was able to save many treasures from being looted. The SS elite front-line troops, on the other hand, had little time for the arts; they were fighting a rearguard action and they took their revenge on their former Italian partners. The Italians themselves were willing to risk their lives for their art treasures, but not to fight any longer for the lost Fascist cause. They were weary of war.

In many cases the Italians succeeded in hiding museum treasures. One British fine arts officer was taken to the Lugolino Golf Club, which had been used by the Germans, and shown the

112

The bridge over the Danube at Linz, in 1943; the only part of Hitler's
original plans that was completed.
The plaster cast model of Kriemhild statue was erected for Hitler's approval.

Above is the architect's model, with (*below*) a detail of one of the statues depicting Kriemhild which, it was said, provided an unusual roosting-place for pigeons.

Göring inspects some scrap metal collected in aid of the war effort in Holland. Note the busts of Hitler and Göring himself.

From the 'Warsaw Accuses' exhibition: the few remaining pieces from the royal castle which was burned by the Nazis.

Some of the main characters in the story:

(*Left*) Ernst Kaltenbrunner, chief of the Reich's main security service, second in command of the SS and Gestapo.

(*Below left*) Gauleiter Josef Bürckel, who from 1938 took charge of Vienna and Lower Austria. He was replaced by Baldur von Schirach and committed suicide in 1944.

(*Below*) Alfred Rosenberg, whose job was to co-ordinate the looting of works of art, particularly from Jewish private collections in France.

(*Right*) The sculptor Graf Plettenburg working on one of the statues which were to be sited on the bridge at Linz. What became of the statues is not known.

Destruction caused by retreating Waffen SS troops at the Chamerolles Château in France.

San Leonardo, Italy: German soldiers unloading works of art looted from the Uffizi Gallery. The painting on its side is Signorelli's *Crucifixion*.

Montegufoni, Italy: treasures from the Uffizi and Pitti Galleries found in Sir George Sitwell's castle.

Professor Michel (seated centre) and Austrian miners who saved a vast hoard of art treasures from being destroyed in the salt-mines at Alt Aussee. Professor Michel is sitting on one of the defused US aerial bombs which the Nazis had placed in the mine.

Two photographs taken inside the mine at Alt Aussee, where the Nazis had hidden thousands of works of art.

entire collection from the Pisa Museum carefully stored in the cavities of partition walls. Private collections were not so lucky: the Finaly Landau collection was seized by the Trettner Parachute Division on the Kunstschutz's orders and sent to the Palazzo Ducale in Bolzano, General Wolff's residence in the South Tyrol. A similar fate befell the Duke of Parma's collection, which was taken by an SS Panzer division and ended up in a castle in Merano. Himmler got to hear of these confiscations and wanted to have some of them transferred to the castle at Wewelsburg, where he too was planning an art centre.

Thanks to Siviero's infiltrators, the MFA&A knew where the truckloads of Florence's art treasures had been taken. The convoys having arrived at San Leonardo and Campo Tures in the South Tyrol, their contents of paintings and sculptures had been hastily unloaded and stacked in a local jail and a castle. What the officers of the MFA&A unit did not know was that both Hitler and Bormann were requesting their immediate dispatch to Germany. General Wolff and Colonel Langsdorff reported to Himmler that this would be impossible: there was no transport or petrol, and the Allies were attacking the rail and road communications through the Brenner Pass. Himmler, however, had his suspicions about General Wolff. It had been reported to him that the general had been in contact with Allied sources in neutral Switzerland. He decided therefore to take no chances and had the general's wife and children taken into custody. Although the entire secret surrender negotiations in Switzerland as well as his life were at stake, Wolff risked going to Berlin to confront both Himmler and his second in command, Kaltenbrunner. He convinced both these men and Hitler that he had only been putting out tentative feelers to ascertain what the Allies had in mind regarding Germany's future. With Hitler's approval, he returned to the South Tyrol, having meanwhile taken his wife and children to safety.

Then came 2nd May, 1945. The German forces under Field-Marshal Kesselring surrendered to Field-Marshal Alexander and his Allied forces. For Italy the war was over. If it had not been for General Wolff's delaying actions in dispatching the works of art from Florence to Bormann in Munich, their eventual fate, in those chaotic days, is anyone's guess. The general, who in fact had no sympathy for the Italians, insisted that he hand them over only to the Allied fine arts officer responsible for the region – a point he had made in his surrender negotiations with Allen Dulles in Switzerland. The last official act carried out by General Wolff was to give Colonel Langsdorff and his assistant their demobilization papers. They reverted to their civilian status as art historians and were appointed by the general as his representatives for the handing over of the Florentine art stores in Campo Tures and San Leonardo to the Americans.

When the Americans representing Dulles arrived from Switzerland they found Wolff's troops still well in control in Bolzano, despite the Germans' surrender. They seemed to believe that they would continue the war against Russia alongside the US Army. It came as a shock to them to realize that they were to be disarmed and sent to prisoner-of-war camps for interrogation.

The US fine arts officers went to San Leonardo, in the remote Passiria valley, and to Campo Tures in the South Tyrol, to recover the Uffizi masterpieces. Among them were Botticelli's *Judith with the Head of Holofernes* and Caravaggio's famous *The Young Bacchus*. Around the damp walls of an old prison courthouse stood Michelangelo sculptures, while Cranach's *Adam* and *Eve* were found wrapped in an old bedspread. It was surprising that some of the pictures were not more damaged, for shortly before the officers arrived at San Leonardo a young woman had come from Munich to photograph them, and apparently, to get better light, she had had them taken out of doors and propped them up in the snow. The photographs had been intended for a presentation album for the Führer's birthday, from which he could make a selection for Linz.

At the other depot, in a castle, conditions had been more favourable, but the officers found a German Panzer regiment stationed in and around it. Tanks were parked there, and a thousand cans of petrol were stacked against the walls, where one cigarette-butt could have sent the whole place up in flames. The troops were much more concerned with their future than with the castle's contents. Among the pictures there were Rubens's *Return of the Peasants*, Donatello's *St George* from the Villa Reale depot in Florence, and many paintings from the Uffizi.

The mixed commission of Italian, British and American officers of the MFA&A had a formidable task in checking the condition of the Florentine art treasures. Almost every item had suffered some kind of damage from the hazards of the trip in unprotected conditions. Only blankets and straw had been used as loose packing, and the straw had tended to scratch the surface of the paintings. Rubens's celebrated *Return of the Peasants* had a blank area where there had been blue sky; the paint had rubbed off against something in transit.

The value of the whole cache of art treasures, according to the American experts, was about $500 million at the end of the war – not such a high figure when it is remembered that it contained the greatest masterpieces of Rubens, Botticelli, Brueghel and Tintoretto, Michelangelo's *Bacchus* and Donatello's *St George*, and many, many other equally famous works. At the Nuremberg War Crimes trial it was stated that the works of art removed by the retreating Germans from Italian museums represented the most important cultural treasure from any of the occupied countries. Today there are still 1,600 items, many very valuable, that have never been found, 600 of them from the Kunstschutz files alone.

The US Fifth Army Arts Division needed nearly two months just to sort out, clean up and crate the works of art handed over by General Wolff's representatives. Then on 20th July, 1945 a special train with thirteen freight trucks arrived at the Campo di Marte station in Florence, loaded with the Uffizi and Pitti treasures from Bolzano. In the Piazza della Signoria, where over 3,000 people had assembled to welcome the return of their treasures, the American General Hume made a short speech on handing them over to the Mayor of Florence. Six token trucks loaded up with the precious cargo and festooned with the flags of Italy and the United States of America drove slowly through the cheering crowds to the steps of the Uffizi. Florence's treasures had come home.

CHAPTER ELEVEN

The Alpine Hoard

The events that led up to the discovery of some of the world's greatest art treasures in the shafts of the ancient salt-mines of Alt Aussee, in Austria, have been documented in the reports of the Allied officers involved. It was not these officers alone who saved Europe's heritage from total destruction, however. Their mission owed much to the courage and initiative of the Austrian miners who helped them.

Researching into these events, I was told in Vienna that I should visit Bad Aussee, the Austrian spa town, where a former Socialist member of the Austrian parliament might be able to help me. The little town, surrounded by high peaks and near to two beautiful Alpine lakes, has an old-world charm. To drive there I went over the Pötschen Pass from Salzburg and checked in at a local hotel. The hotelier was somewhat surprised to have a visitor arrive out of season, and even more so when I asked to be put through on the telephone to my contact, Herr Nationalrat Gaiswinkler. It was only later that I realized why. In 1965 Nazi sympathies were still in evidence. Why was an Englishman, speaking fluent German with a Viennese accent, asking for a Socialist party member? Under the surface of this peaceful place there was an odd atmosphere, and I had the feeling of being an unwelcome visitor who had come to disturb past history.

The gist of the story had already been explained to me in Vienna by Dr Dworschak of the Kunsthistorisches Museum. In

124

1942 some shafts of the disused salt-mine at Alt Aussee had been inspected with a view to their being utilized as a storehouse for works of art. It was noticed during the inspection that, in a small chapel hewn out of the salt rock wall of a cave, the wooden altar-piece and decorations of green fir were in perfect condition through they had been neglected for years. The steady temperature and the right degree of humidity made the mine an ideal storage place. Subsequently electric lighting was installed and wooden tiers were erected to hold the paintings. As soon as the storehouse was ready, the most valuable of the works from the Vienna museums were packed into it, safe from the Allied bombing. As the air attacks increased, Hitler needed a safer depository for his Linz collection, which was then in Munich, and he commandeered the Alt Aussee storehouse exclusively for his own use. By 1944 Alt Aussee had become his main depository for all the art treasures looted from Europe. Hofrat Professor Michel, an elderly museum curator from Vienna, was in charge of conservation.

I first met Herr Nationalrat Albrecht Gaiswinkler in the garden of a local inn. I was surprised to be greeted by a tall, athletic, good-looking man in his late fifties with greying hair. His tanned face showed him to be a mountaineer. The following is the story of Alt Ausee as it was related to me by him.

While working locally as a clerk in the government health insurance office Herr Gaiswinkler had got involved in organizing anti-Nazi sympathizers. The authorities began to suspect him, and to avoid imprisonment he joined the Luftwaffe. He was sent to Normandy, where he was soon able to make contact with the local Maquis. From his letters from home, meanwhile, he learnt that weekly convoys of trucks stacked with wooden crates were seen driving through the village at night in the direction of the salt-mines. The area had been placed out of bounds to the villagers and was guarded by heavily armed SS men. The Alt Aussee salt-mines, Herr Gaiswinkler explained, had been in use since Roman times and were still in operation. Another unexplained mystery was that often the local inhabitants had heard loud explosions coming from the direction of Lake Töplitz, situated in the vicinity.

When the Allies landed in southern France Gaiswinkler found himself left in charge of twenty-five men, the troops having been moved to the front to fight the invaders. He seized the chance to desert to the Maquis. While he was with the Maquis a report was sent to London mentioning that he had information which might be of value to the war effort. He was then smuggled across to the Allied lines and brought over to England to be interrogated under cover of secrecy at a house near Reading. He told his interrogators that, according to his miner friends at home, vast quantities of art treasures were being stacked in the Alt Aussee salt-mines on specially constructed shelves. Many works from the Vienna museums had already been deposited there, and new stuff was being secretly brought in all the time. He also told them that he thought Hitler's armies might make a last stand in that corner of the Austrian Alps, no definite information concerning this was available to the Supreme Command of Allied Forces in Europe.

Gaiswinkler was asked if he would be prepared to undergo a sabotage training course and then be dropped in his home area. His task would be to organize local resistance, report on German Army concentrations in the area, and ascertain what was happening at the salt-mines and Lake Töplitz. Gaiswinkler accepted. After six months of intensive training, during which he was not allowed to speak any German, he was flown out under the name of Major Thomas to the British air base at Brindisi on the Adriatic. Here he joined forces with three other Austrians, one of them a radio operator. By now, much of Italy had been taken by the Allies and they were surging on towards Germany. Rumours about Hitler's last stand in the *Alpenfestung* (Alpine fortress) in the mountains were circulating. The American fine arts officers had been told by a captured German art historian who had worked with the ERR in Paris that looted art treasures had been deposited in castles in Bavaria and Austria, and that some had gone to the salt-mines of Alt Aussee.

There was no time to be lost. Gaiswinkler's group had twice been taken by air to the dropping zone, but on account of bad visibility had had to return to base in Italy. On the third attempt weather conditions were suitable for the parachute drop, but unfortunately the plane overshot the point where local Resistance workers were waiting, and the four found themselves on a snow-covered slope in the Höllengebirge Mountains, not far from the edge of a precipice. Up to his armpits in snow, Gaiswinkler fortunately recognized where they were – miles from their destination, and high above the notorious Ebensee concentration camp.

The Gestapo, having learnt that agents had been dropped in the mountains, had sent out search parties. However, after a series of adventurous escapes the four reached Bad Aussee on a local train from Ebensee, jumping off before it reached the station. The whole area in early 1945 was teeming with Nazi refugees billeted with local families. The German Foreign Office had been evacuated here, as well as the puppet governments of Serbia, Croatia, Hungary and Bulgaria, complete with their gold reserves and foreign currencies. The remnants of the German Balkan armies under General Fabianku had been ordered to withdraw to this Alpine retreat and defend it. The Gestapo and the SS were on the look-out for spies and saboteurs, and mobile courts martial were summarily ordering the execution of anyone suspected of anti-Nazi sympathies.

Gaiswinkler's group found their transmitter had been irreparably damaged on landing. However, Gaiswinkler learnt from friends in the local Resistance that there was a double agent in Bad Aussee working with the Americans. He turned out to be an SD operator attached to Kaltenbrunner, second in command under Himmler of the SS and the Gestapo, and also known as 'little Himmler'. Gaiswinkler could hardly believe this – but it was true. He provided him with a spare transmitter and enabled him to contact his British base. Gaiswinkler found the local Resistance splintered into a number of small groups and very disorganized. With the help of his three companions he organized them into an effective unit under his command as Major T.

From the salt-mines the miners reported the arrival of more and more convoys of art works. The two men in charge of the depository, Hofrat Professor Michel and a Herr Karl Sieber, a German art restorer, had by now been recruited into the Resistance group and were able to give valuable information.

A young boy brought Gaiswinkler a message from the miners that a mysterious convoy heavily guarded by SS men had arrived at the mine. It consisted of six large wooden crates marked MARMOR NICHT STÜRZEN (Marble Do Not Drop). Supervised by the local Nazi leader and his immediate superior, the regional inspector for the Upper Region, Herr Glinz, they had to load the crates on to the mine trolleys, a job that required a number of men as they were very heavy. What puzzled the men was that the explosives expert and director of mines, Herr Kain, was also present, and that SS men were guarding the entrance to the mine. The loaded trolleys were carefully pushed along a narrow-gauge track to the entrance of the main shaft. What their contents were was a mystery, even to the mining officials.

Gaiswinkler issued immediate instructions to the miners to try to find out what was in the crates. During a night shift two of the miners succeeded in forcing one of them open. Inside was a 500-pound unexploded US-made aerial bomb. They reported their discovery at once to Professor Michel, who now realized the sinister intentions of the SS. Six such bombs were more than enough to blow up the entire mine and its contents.

It was very important meanwhile not to arouse the SS guards' suspicions. Gaiswinkler's group kept a watch on the mine area from the surrounding woods; the miners armed themselves and kept a constant check inside the mine. Professor Michel learnt by devious means that the proposed destruction had been ordered by a high authority, though he could not discover whether this was the Führer himself.

In the bowels of the mine, in a large cave, was the chapel dedicated to the miners' patron saint, St Leonhard. As the atmosphere there was ideal for storage, Michel decided to transfer the most valuable of the works of art to the chapel. At night, by the light of two miners' lamps, the transfer began. Michel had two helpers, as well as his girl assistant who was also official photographer of the art works. The first pieces to be taken down slippery steps hewn out of the salt rock were the Ghent altar panels. Through the night the group worked to salvage the masterpieces; but what they did not take into account was the existence of a stagnant lake within the mountain above the chapel. If in fact there had been an explosion the entire ceiling would have caved in under the pressure of the water and everything would have been destroyed.

Meanwhile the local gendarmerie had joined the Resistance and supplied firearms and ammunition. Dressed in German officers' uniforms, Gaiswinkler's men gave orders to the retreating troops, who then found themselves trapped and disarmed by the Resistance men. Gaiswinkler's group became somewhat worried about the number of war-weary German troops they were disarming; it needed perhaps only one tough Nazi officer to appear on the scene for the tables to be turned.

In fact this is what nearly did happen. The group heard that Otto Skorzeny, the Nazi commander who undertook the daring air rescue of Mussolini from a mountain fortress in Italy, was advancing on them with a force of 800 SS troops for the purpose of wiping out any resistance. Quick thinking by Gaiswinkler saved the day. The rumour was spread that Tito's partisans were planning a parachute drop. Armoured cars that had been taken from the retreating troops of the German 6th Army were equipped with the red-and-white Austrian colours. Suddenly confronted by them and thinking there were more to follow, Skorzeny and his troops quickly retreated.

Meanwhile at his villa in Alt Aussee Kaltenbrunner, second in command of the SS and Gestapo, was contacted by Gauleiter Eigruber, who was in charge of Upper Austria and under whose jurisdiction the area fell. Thanks to the wife of a local doctor, Gaiswinkler got possession of the official Gestapo rubber stamp without which no document was valid in the area, and by a clever ruse enticed Eigruber's personal assistant and three leading Gestapo officials to a night rendezvous, where they were 'arrested' by the Resistance and taken in their own car to a secret hide-out. There a mock court martial was staged and immediate sentence of death pronounced. Realizing that the war was rapidly coming to an end, the prisoners offered to co-operate with the Resistance in return for their lives.

Gaiswinkler had to decide whether or not he could trust them. They could easily betray him to Kaltenbrunner, who would then take immediate action against the Resistance, but Gaiswinkler decided to take the gamble. The men were Austrians, not Germans; and besides, they were well aware that things were not going their way. They genuinely believed him to be a British officer.

As it happened, the gamble paid off handsomely. The Gestapo officials, remaining in their jobs, not only passed on to Gaiswinkler the secret communications going to and from Kaltenbrunner's headquarters but supplied him with copies of all orders issued by Eigruber. It was Eigruber who had received the instructions to place the bombs in the salt-mine and who had supplied the fuses for the final explosion. Who gave the instructions in the first place – Hitler, Bormann, or possibly Himmler – I have not been able to establish from the available documents. Whoever it was, Eigruber was determined that the art treasures should not fall into what he called 'Jewish or Bolshevik' hands.

Gaiswinkler was living in the woods in a shed; he could not let himself be seen in the village or he would have been recognized at once. Officially he was still a prisoner of war of the British. Only at night could he risk visiting his father's house, where he would hold meetings with the other Resistance members. His son brought food to his hide-out, a number of schoolchildren being used as couriers by their anti-Nazi parents. Other members of his group, as well as army deserters, were also hiding out in the hills. It was April 1945 and Germany was losing the war. The whole Aussee region was in a turmoil. Kaltenbrunner and other Nazi leaders had taken refuge there from the Allied forces, which were advancing from all sides. The Nazi propaganda machine was exploiting the notion of an Alpine fortress. Everyone was beginning to believe in this last refuge of Nazism, but in fact there was not one fortified position in the Alpine area.

German troops were pouring back over the Pötschen Pass into Germany in their hundreds. Gaiswinkler and his group, armed as they were, were greatly outnumbered. Their only means of survival was bluff. The rumour spread that Tito's forces, who were greatly feared for their ferocity, had infiltrated the surrounding mountains. Gaiswinkler got his men to light fires on the mountain tops to indicate signalling. The order of the day was to create confusion. Indeed confusion reigned everywhere. The Americans had reached Salzburg, and the Russians were in Linz, which was already divided by the Danube into Soviet and American zones. Hitler's birthplace had offered no resistance. A free Austrian radio had been established. In the nearby castle of Teisch a powerful relay transmitter, captured from the Nazis by the local Austrian Resistance, was used for liberation broadcasts.

At the mine, time was running out and the miners decided to take action themselves. They knew that the detonators for the bombs were also stored in the mine. They suggested to Professor Michel that they blast all but the main entrance to the mine with small charges that would block free passage to, but not damage the interior, and, desperate as he was, Michel agreed to their suggestion. Gaiswinkler meanwhile had heard from his agents that orders had come from Eigruber and Kaltenbrunner to blow up the mine, and that a special demolition squad of reliable SS men had already been detailed to carry out this task. He decided on immediate action. He telephoned Kaltenbrunner and told him the order must be countermanded. When Kaltenbrunner refused, one of his aides – now in the Resistance – persuaded him to change his mind. Kaltenbrunner countermanded the order.

The miners at once moved the bombs out of the mine into a nearby field. But neither they nor Gaiswinkler trusted the Nazis. Eigruber by now knew of Kaltenbrunner's betrayal. Conditions at this time were too chaotic for him to get orders from Hitler in his Berlin bunker, so he ordered a demolition squad of SS men from Innsbruck. Meanwhile much destruction was going on in the Aussee area. The Villa Castiglione on the nearby Grundl Lake was threatened. The villa had been used as a summer residence for Nazi officials, including Goebbels and his family, and contained the greater part of Hitler's Linz library. The SS had orders to demolish it, but a last-minute struggle by armed Resistance fighters saved it from destruction.

The German 6th Army, still intact but without any orders from the Führer, had poured into the area under its commander General Fabianku. Gaiswinkler's group was getting bolder all the time, and the general ordered a raid on their headquarters. But against the determined armed Resistance fighters the attack by the demoralized Germans failed. One of Gaiswinkler's couriers was arrested, however, and sent by Fabianku to Mittendorf to be shot. Then in a bold daylight raid General Fabianku was himself kidnapped and taken to Gaiswinkler's headquarters. Unless their man was released, Fabianku was told, he would be shot. Fabianku ordered the prisoner's release.

It was now that a further series of loud explosions was heard from the direction of Lake Töplitz. This time Gaiswinkler's group were able to discover the cause: based there was a research station for the development of sonic mines and torpedoes, and as well as being evacuated it was being blown up.

Two of the Aussee Resistance men, having forged documents for themselves with Gestapo rubber stamps and notepaper, succeeded in getting through to the American command in Vöcklabruck where they reported the dangerous situation of the art stores in the mine. When the Americans advanced on the area,

Gaiswinkler and his men drove up to the Pötschen Pass in a tank and an armoured vehicle to welcome them. The Americans were impressed by this, and seeing that the area was already liberated were in no hurry to move in. The three days until they finally did so were something of a nightmare for the Resistance group. What would they do if some tough SS regiment suddenly appeared on the scene? German troops were continually drifting through the area – about 6,000, according to Gaiswinkler, though most of them were anxious only to escape home without encountering the Russians or the Yugoslav partisans who they believed were in the vicinity.

All over the countryside there were displaced persons roaming free and taking revenge on the Germans for their years of forced labour, or else just out to loot whatever they could lay their hands on. There were armed groups of SS men in the mountains too. At the mine, however, troops of the US 80th Infantry Division had been placed on guard and, with the arrival of the fine arts officer, Captain Posey, and his assistant, Private Kirstein, the evacuation of the art treasures was to be the next move.

Professor Michel, helped by Herr Sieber, had kept careful records of the condition and whereabouts of the stores, and thanks to them these had suffered little damage. For Captain Posey, the discovery of the Van Eyck altar-piece and the Madonna from Bruges was the end of a determined search for these treasures. In addition, stacked away in the mine, were the imperial crown and all the regalia of the Austrian Empire, while in another mine nearby strong-boxes containing $4\frac{1}{2}$ million Reichsmarks of army funds were found. Other discoveries were made. In the garden of the Villa Kerry, Kaltenbrunner's headquarters, about 75 kilograms (165 lb) of gold coins of different currencies and a number of gold bars were unearthed; and then vast quantities of army stores came to light – 80,000 kilograms (176,400 lb) of sugar, 75,000 tins of sardines and canned meat, quantities of tobacco and cigarettes, plus about 80,000 kilograms of shoe-leather. Lastly, the secret correspondence between Seyss-Inquart and Bormann was found, and this was used by the prosecution at the Nuremberg trial. The number of hoarded art treasures was staggering. There were more than 6,500 paintings earmarked for the Führermuseum in Linz, mainly valuable Old Masters; sculptures, historic coin collections and tapestries, together with

innumerable prints and drawings; plus armour looted from the
Naples Museum as well as the Gordon Craig theatre archives confiscated in France. All this was quite apart from the legitimately
stored works of art from Vienna's museums.

There remained, for me, a mystery about the wartime events at
Lake Töplitz, near Bad Aussee. This small mountain lake of deep
green, almost black, water is surrounded by steep cliffs crowned
by pine forests. As I was taken round it in a small motorboat it
was explained to me that over the centuries tree-trunks had
crashed into it and formed a kind of waterlogged floating island in
its depths. At the far end there were large concrete blocks leaning
drunkenly into the water, the remains of the research station for
underwater missiles that the retreating Germans had blown up.

The enigma of Lake Töplitz, which years later caused a murder
and two deaths, developed in the last days of World War II. It was
in the middle of the night, Herr Gaiswinkler told me, that two
local farmers in his Resistance group were hauled out of their beds
by SS men and told to bring out a horse and cart. They drove the
cart up to an army truck loaded with wooden boxes of various
sizes and transferred the cargo to the cart, then on the Germans'
instructions they took the cart along a track that was too narrow
for trucks to the lake. When they got there they found a small
boat waiting for them. They loaded their cargo on to the boat, and
through the night they drove to and from the lake until they had
transferred all the wooden boxes. Then in the faint light of dawn
they observed the boxes being tipped over the side of the boat into
the depths of the lake. They had seen enough. They decided there
and then to leave the farmhouse and go into hiding in the woods
with other Resistance fighters, before the SS shot them as wit-
nesses.

I wanted to know more about the background to this escapade,
and Herr Gaiswinkler suggested I contact a Dr Wilhelm Hoettl,
who ran a small school in the neighbourhood. Hoettl had been
involved with Heydrich and Kaltenbrunner, and I might learn
more from him. As it happened, I had an Austrian friend whose
son had been at the school and who could give me an introduc-
tion. I telephoned Dr Hoettl and explained about my research,
and he agreed to see me.

At the school, housed in a chalet on a hill some distance from
Bad Aussee and guarded by a fierce Alsatian dog, Dr Hoettl filled

in more of the story.

Hoettl had been attached to the foreign section of the Sicher-heitsdienst or SD which was part of Heydrich's set-up under Himmler. The SD was a spy network within the Party itself, and its purpose was to feed information back to Himmler. In Germany it consisted of thousands of informers from all walks of life, as well as professional members. The SD worked hand in glove with the Gestapo, and no organization or individual was safe from it. Anyone revealing hostility to the regime was immediately reported and lost his job.

Hoettl had been involved by Heydrich in a lawsuit, and as a punishment he was sent in 1941 to the Russian Front. After Heydrich's assassination in Prague by Czech commandos sent over from Britain, Hoettl was reinstated under the new chief, Walter Schellenberg. His operational area was south-east Europe and Italy. In 1944, working from Budapest, Hoettl realized the war was as good as lost. Daily reports were coming in to the Hungarian Ministry of War and the SS headquarters; a private conversation with Eichmann confirmed the situation for Hoettl. Unknown to the Nazi authorities, he contacted Allen Dulles's secret headquarters – the Office of Strategic Services (OSS) – in Berne, Switzerland, which recruited foreign agents and chan-nelled information to the supreme commander of the Allied forces.

It was in March 1945, Hoettl told me, that he moved his family to Bad Aussee. Through the intelligence link with Dulles in Switzerland he knew Austria was going to be split into four sec-tions at the end of the war, and he realized that if he or his family stayed in the Vienna area they could be in a Russian zone. What he did not know, however, was that in the Aussee area he would find himself in the thick of things.

Some time after arriving there he was contacted by Gais-winkler, who knew of his presence. He met Gaiswinkler in his hide-out and was asked to convey a message to the Americans that the area should not be bombed, even though it was – mistakenly – believed to be the site where the Nazi High Command was going to make its last stand. Under the Germans the Aussee region had been made part of the Upper Danube area under Gauleiter Eigruber, rather than remaining part of Styria, and by this odd chance would come under American occupation. Eigruber was a Nazi extremist, Hoettl pointed out, who would stop at nothing to prevent the treasures in the salt-mine from falling into the Allies' hands. But for Hitler, on the other hand, it was the greatest of his ambitions to preserve them for the Linz Museum. This, Hoettl believed, was why in spite of his intransigence in defeat Hitler never ordered their destruction.

Just how desperately Hitler clung to his plan for Linz is shown by a story that Kaltenbrunner related to Hoettl. In 1945, convinced that the war was lost, Kaltenbrunner had visited Hitler in his Berlin bunker to advise him to resign and appoint representatives to sign a cease-fire. Hitler sensed that one of his most faithful followers was weakening. He told Kaltenbrunner to attend the next military briefing at midday and come to see him afterwards. When Kaltenbrunner arrived, Hitler took him into a small room. Before he had a chance to discuss the military situation, Hitler started to talk about the plans for Linz – which was also Kaltenbrunner's birthplace. He asked Kaltenbrunner about where the bridges across the Danube should be built, where certain heavy industrial plants should be sited. Then suddenly he turned to face Kaltenbrunner. 'My dear Kaltenbrunner,' he exclaimed, 'if both of us were not convinced that after the victorious conclusion of the war we would build this new Linz together, I would shoot myself today.' Kaltenbrunner was speechless. He left the Führer in the bunker with his illusions, never to see him alive again. A few weeks later Hitler did shoot himself.

What was the truth about the odd activities at Lake Töplitz, I asked Hoettl? In 1945 the story behind the dumping of the boxes in the deep green waters of the lake was still obscure. A few years after the war, Hoettl said, fishermen on the lake noticed a steady stream of banknotes floating to the surface. On closer inspection, these proved to be five-, ten- and twenty-pound sterling notes. The police were alerted; bank officials were called in. The notes, after careful checking, proved to be fakes. Hoettl found himself confronted by his former wartime activities and was able to throw some light on the story.

It was Heydrich who had proposed to Hitler that they flood non-belligerent countries with faked English money in order to ruin the British economy abroad. Hitler had endorsed the idea and Hoettl, among others, had been involved in its execution. The most accomplished forgers, many of them in German gaols and concentration camps, were rounded up and eventually placed under strict guard in a camp near Ebensee. They were well looked after and given every possible facility for their work. In his facinating book *Hitler's Paper War* (1955) Hoettl has described how the forgers were able to produce almost faultless notes which only the Bank of England could detect as fakes. When the American forces were advancing on the area it became imperative to hide the printing-plates and all the evidence – and the nearest lake that was considered deep enough was Töplitz. Over the years the wooden boxes became waterlogged and the notes inside swelled and burst the boxes.

The Töplitz story made headlines around the world. Divers have since searched the lake and brought up material that was immediately impounded by the Austrian police. Much speculation followed. Some newspapers claimed the divers had found secret files on leading Austrian Nazis, others that they had brought up forged dollar notes, but the truth has never been revealed.

The rumour that there was still loot to be found in this remote spot persisted, but various attempts by amateur divers to find it failed. One diver became entangled in the layer of waterlogged tree-trunks below the surface and died. And there have been two unsolved murders in the woods that surround the lake.

Through Herr Gaiswinkler I met some of the surviving miners of Alt Aussee. The meeting took place in the garden of the inn at Eselsbach, where Gaiswinkler was living. Sitting round the table with us, these now elderly men admitted that they had been less concerned with the heroic aspect of saving the art treasures than with preserving their own livelihood. For generations the salt-mines had provided employment, for rock-salt was always in great demand. If the mines of Alt Aussee had been destroyed it would have been the end of a profitable local industry. Of the others involved in the preservation of the Aussee hoard, Professor Michel had since died and all that was left was for me to collect from his widow in Vienna some photographs of the interior of the mine, with its precious contents stacked in wooden compartments. The whereabouts of his assistant, the picture restorer Sieber, was not known. Herr Gaiswinkler, whose last minute actions were instrumental in saving Europe's greatest art treasures from final destruction, died a few years ago.

CHAPTER TWELVE

The Aftermath

Once the war was over the American art-looting investigation unit of the Office of Strategic Services set up an interrogation centre at Alt Aussee. There the principals involved in Special Mission Linz were brought from custody to be interrogated. Among them were Haberstock, buyer for both Hitler and Göring, Andreas Hofer, Katejan Mühlmann, Heinrich Hoffman, and Göring's private secretary, Fräulein Limberger. The German art dealers in Munich and other cities who had been involved in the project were also questioned, though none was actually prosecuted.

The detailed card index of the works destined for Linz was held at Schloss Weesenstein, near Dresden, which unfortunately was in Soviet hands, and the Russians refused to release it. When they occupied Dresden they removed the entire remaining collection from the town's museum to Leningrad, and no doubt the card index as well as the Weesenstein treasures ended up there. But investigators found that in the Führerbau in Munich the record of all items received, carefully maintained by Dr Reger, had not been disturbed by the Munich mob that had been looting and running wild ever since the Nazi guards fled.

The task that awaited the MFA&A at the end of the war was immensely complex; they had to list and trace innumerable works of art throughout Europe. All the art commissions were confronted with chaotic conditions, and the farther the Allied forces penetrated into Germany the greater had been the confusion. The 'fine arts boys', as the Americans called them, faced a formidable job. By this time they were no longer attached to fighting units but had become a most important peacetime force. One factor that affected their task was that the Germans had not taken the evacuation of many of their own art treasures seriously until towards the end of the war. They deposited some works in their flak-towers* but resisted the pleas of the museum authorities to organize a full evacuation, fearing to disturb popular morale. Eventually, when the Allied troops were almost on top of them, the Germans roughly packed and deposited the major part of the collections in places totally unprepared to receive them. Unbelievable as it may seem, collections from the important Berlin museums were evacuated from the flak-towers to the country only weeks before the city capitulated. Professor Webb of the Macmillan Fine Arts commission recalled how more and more rumours of hidden works of art kept reaching them. Various farms and country houses were found stacked with pictures, a valuable Gothic painting being discovered in a small house in Westphalia.

The MFA&A established central collecting-points, the two most important ones being in Wiesbaden and in Munich, in the American zone of occupation. Each country had appointed someone to be responsible for the fine arts, and these officers helped the American team identify each item's country of origin. In Munich it was the Führerbau that was used as a collecting-point, and with its cellars and many spacious rooms it proved ideal for the purpose. All Germans working there were vetted, and the truckloads of works of art that poured in were strictly guarded.

The locations of the various hide-outs, most of them known only to Nazi-employed personnel, had to be traced. But many Nazi officials had gone into hiding with their leaders, and there was considerable anxiety meanwhile about the activities of

---

* A flak-tower was a building with a high concrete tower which, apart from acting as a bomb shelter below, had on its rooftop anti-aircraft guns. It was one of Hitler's main defences against Allied air raids, and afforded a clear view above a city's skyline of approaching enemy aircraft. Placed in important defensive positions in German cities, these near-indestructible buildings are still in existence and are used now for storage of goods.

marauding bands of ex-prisoners of war as well as of displaced persons set free from forced labour camps. They took anything that caught their fancy in abandoned houses, irrespective of its value, often throwing it away later if it proved difficult to carry.

The most disastrous incident occurred at the Friedrichshain flak-tower in Berlin. Collections from the Berlin museums had been stored in this tower in the city centre, and when the MFA&A teams arrived after the city's final capitulation they found it unguarded. But displaced persons had sheltered there and had apparently lit a fire, which spread through one floor of the building and destroyed over 400 pictures of the Italian School, some Van Dyck paintings, valuable sculptures, historic textiles, furniture and glass. In another part of the building, however, some works of art remained undamaged. As the tower was in the Soviet-occupied zone, Russian troops took all that was left back to their country; and then in the course of this removal another fire broke out that destroyed yet more treasures. Altogether, as far as the figurative arts were concerned, this was the greatest disaster since the Palace and Alcazar of Madrid were destroyed in 1734.

It was not until late in 1944 that military transport was provided to evacuate what remained of the contents of Berlin's Kaiser Friedrich Museum. Conditions by this time were desperately difficult, but through the last-minute efforts of the devoted museum staff and with the help of art students the collections reached a salt-mine in Westphalia. When Professor Webb's investigating officer arrived there he found great heaps of fur coats that had been destined for the Russian front being rifled by displaced persons and freed Russian prisoners. When they had cleared everyone out of the mine, the MFA&A officers discovered, buried below the pile of coats, stocks of gold from the Reichsbank in Berlin, large quantities of hock, and the Kaiser Friedrich Museum collections.

Then, in a farmhouse in Westphalia, not far from the twelfth-century Wewelsburg Castle housing the SS school that trained future Nazi leaders, the British MFA&A officers discovered Himmler's hoard. It included an assortment of antique cutlery, Russian paintings and superb antique armoury, some bought in Holland and France, which were evidently his particular collecting interests. There was also a magnificent 18-inch high silver-gilt cup inscribed with the arms of the third Baron Foley, under the rim of which was an 1816 hallmark and the inscription 'Chelmsford Races'. Where Himmler obtained this piece remains a mystery. His collection of paintings, apart from the Russian pictures and a Teniers, was made up of the mediocre productions of Nazi artists. Among other curiosities found in the farmhouse were antique torture instruments, ancient documents from the city of Münster, and a complete set of modern dental instruments.

Not far from Wewelsburg Castle there was a concentration camp, from which, following the collapse of the Nazi regime, the inmates flocked into the countryside in search of food, clothes and revenge. Many of them returned to the camp loaded with loot from nearby castles and villas: Flemish tapestries, Dutch Old Master paintings and carpets. Among the prisoners there had been 250 theological students, twenty-five of whom were still alive, and these few appealed successfully to the unruly mob to deposit their loot in the only available storeroom in the camp, the laundry-room. Thus, when the MFA&A officers arrived, they found the room stacked with the pilfered works of art. It was these same students who had seen to it that Himmler's hoard remained untouched and had rescued all the SS school records after part of the castle had been blown up by the retreating SS demolition squad.

In the Bernterode mines in Westphalia a somewhat macabre discovery was made. These mines had been used since 1936 for the storage of high explosives from a nearby munitions plant, and consisted of twenty-three interconnected passages 1,650 feet underground. They had been staffed by slave labour. Forty thousand tons of ammunition, as well as quantities of dynamite, were found by the Allied forces that captured the place. When the MFA&A men came in to explore the various tunnels they reached a walled-up section. On breaking through it they found themselves in a large cave. Stacked round it were paintings, sealed boxes and military banners, and in the centre were four coffins. The coffins were decorated with wreaths and red silk ribbons embossed with the swastika and Hitler's name, and on each a scribbled note in red pencil was attached with tape. These were the names recorded there: Frederick William I, Frederick (II) the Great (both kings of Prussia), Field-Marshal von Hindenburg and Frau von Hindenburg. The 200 banners strung around the cave represented regiments from early Prussian times up to the

1914–18 war. In three bays of the cave there were portraits that had been taken from the Sans-Souci Palace at Potsdam, together with tapestries and the crown jewels of Prussia, including a richly jewelled sceptre and orb, two crowns and two swords with finely wrought gold and silver scabbards. According to eyewitness accounts, these national treasures had been brought to the mine by military personnel under conditions of great secrecy. The MFA&A officers had a dangerous task here, since before touching anything else they had to move great quantities of volatile high explosives. I was never able to establish whether, as some maintained, Hitler had intended to blow the whole place up, or whether it had been Himmler's idea of a secret shrine, known only to a few of the Nazi hierarchy and not to be resurrected until the revival of the Fourth Reich.

Another very important find was that of the insignia of the Holy Roman Empire. These had been removed by the Nazis from Vienna to Nuremberg in 1938. When the Americans reached Nuremberg and interrogated the local Nazi bosses they were told by them that the insignia had been taken away by an unknown high-ranking SS officer and sunk in the Zell am See Lake in Austria. The investigating officers were not satisfied with this story and after fruitless attempts to elicit the truth decided on more drastic methods. Thus it was that the Mayor of Nuremberg was arrested and told he was to be confronted with a Sicherheitsdienst official who would implicate him. Under this pressure the mayor admitted that he had had the insignia placed in specially made copper containers and walled up in the underground corridor of the Paniers Platz bunker in Nuremberg, in the presence of three other Nazi officials. Drilling through concrete in a room 80 feet below ground level, the American fine arts officers found a small cavity containing the undamaged containers. The insignia were returned to Vienna. It was Himmler, apparently, who had ordered that they be walled up and had instructed Kaltenbrunner to spread the story of their disposal in the lake. But for the Americans' investigations in this matter, today's visitors to the Schatzkammer (Treasure Chamber) in the Vienna Hofburg would not be able to see Europe's most historic imperial relics.

From the American investigators' reports it appeared that Bavaria was considered by the Nazi chiefs to be the safest haven for their loot. It was in Ehrenbreitstein in Bavaria that the paintings and archives of the Dutch royal family were discovered. At Neuhaus the former Nazi governor-general of Poland, Hans Frank, had secreted the treasures he looted from that country. Among them was the famous *Lady with a Weasel* which Dr Posse had originally earmarked for Linz, but which for some unknown reason was rejected. When it was sent back to Warsaw Frank took it for his residence in Cracow.

When the American fine arts officers appeared on the scene Frank made an unsuccessful attempt at suicide. As it turned out, he was one of the surviving Nazi leaders to appear in the dock at the Nuremberg trial, and among the evidence produced by the American prosecutor was a printed catalogue of his art thefts. Frank even claimed that the *Lady with a Weasel*, though originally stolen, had been a personal present to him from the Führer. He ended his life on the gallows.

Hitler's main 'safe' depository for art treasures looted from France was the romantic castle of Neuschwanstein in the Bavarian Alps near Füssen. Surrounded by high mountains, this dream castle was built by the 'mad' King Ludwig II of Bavaria, a great patron of the arts in the nineteenth century and a personal friend of Wagner. It was designed as a monument to the composer, and the spacious hall of the castle is decorated with scenes from Wagner's operas. A special concert hall was built there for performances of his music. King Ludwig's philosophy of Pan-Germanism and his admiration for Wagner had Hitler's wholehearted approval, and having visited Neuschwanstein several times Hitler was in no doubt that the castle was ideal for storing his loot. Tucked away as it was in a valley among the mountains, it would be safe from Allied air attacks. At Neuschwanstein the art commission found approximately 6,000 paintings as well as sculptures, silver and a collection of rare books – over 21,000 objects in all. Everything had been carefully documented and indexed as confiscated by the ERR in Paris from the Rothschild family and other Jewish owners of art collections. It took over four months to sort through all the contents and dispatch the first consignment in eighteen fully loaded wagons back to the original owners in Paris, over 200 of them.

In the old monastery buildings at Buxheim, in the same area, the commission found a hoard of abandoned works of art in damp unheated rooms. One room contained damaged paintings and broken wood-carvings, silver and glass. It had been the repair shop for objects that had been damaged in transit from France, and the restorers had fled and left everything lying around. In another room there were 200 paintings that had been looted from Russian museums, alongside which was the royal Bavarian collection from Munich, which had been hastily evacuated when Allied air attacks on the city began.

When the US 101st Armoured Division and the French Armoured Division swept into Berchtesgaden, where Hitler and Göring had their country homes – Hitler's was the famous Eagle's Nest, situated on a mountain top – they stumbled across valuable art treasures in the office of a local Nazi officer and grocer, dumped in piles and stacked against wash-basins. Then, on a railway siding and half in a tunnel, they found an abandoned train, some of the freight cars of which had been broken into. Inside they found works of art. The hastily alerted fine arts officers at once placed everything under guard. Not until Andreas Hofer, Göring's art adviser, gave himself up did they realize that all this was part of the Reichsmarschall's fabulous collection from Karinhall. Hofer explained that, as the Soviet armies advanced through East Prussia, Göring had ordered the evacuation of most of his Karinhall collection. It went first to his house in Berlin, was moved from there to his estate at Veldenstein because of air attacks, and then finally was moved on to Berchtesgaden. Göring himself, returning to Berchtesgaden from his last visit to Hitler at the end of April 1945, was arrested by a special SS detachment. The Führer had branded him a traitor, stripped him of all his titles, and appointed Admiral Dönitz in his place.* Together with some of his tapestries and paintings Göring was taken by the SS to Mauterndorf, and it was here that the Americans eventually caught up with him. Hofer reported that some 600–1,000 paintings and about eighty sculptures had been on the train. Some of the freight cars had been sent down the line to the small station of Unterstein, and there the American fine arts officers under Captain Anderson continued their search. One large freight car

* Hitler's action was the result of Martin Bormann's intrigues against Göring. According to Albert Speer, Göring had merely asked Hitler whether he should assume leadership of the Reich if the Führer remained incarcerated in his Berlin bunker. However, Bormann craftily managed to convince Hitler that Göring was staging a *coup d'état*.

was found to be full of books and papers. In another siding were freight cars that had been broken into by the local people, but fortunately many of the objects taken were found later in private houses nearby. The Gestapo had also helped themselves. In another part of the train the Americans discovered the best part of Göring's private wine cellar from Karinhall, with some of the cases broken open.

When I visited the site in 1965 I was told by an elderly porter that he remembered how the soldiers guarding the train went on a drinking spree once they heard that Göring had been arrested, and that when the first American troops arrived they found them sleeping off their hangovers.

A sequel to this incident is mentioned in one of the American interrogation reports. Göring, to begin with, was entertained courteously by the Allied generals interrogating him, since they hoped to get information out of him. However, although the ex-Reichsmarschall was too wily to be caught out in this way, what he did not realize was that the excellent champagne he was offered came from his own hoard on the Berchtesgaden train.

Göring agreed at a preliminary interrogation to list all the works of art he had acquired through the ERR confiscations in Paris so that they could be returned to their owners. His entire collection went to the Americans' collecting-point in Munich to be sorted out. Meanwhile his wife Emmy was being interrogated in Zell am See in Austria. She had a number of pictures in her own possession, among them the famous 'Vermeer', *Christ and the Woman Taken in Adultery*, for which Göring had paid 1,600,000 Dutch guilders in Holland. The fact that this painting proved to be a fake needs some explanation.

After the liberation of the Netherlands, the Dutch Government investigation authorities looking into art deals during the Occupation came across the accounts of the Goudstikker Art Gallery. Among them was a receipt for a Vermeer sold to one of Göring's buyers. The vendor was a certain Van Meegeren. Since even during the war it was prohibited for the Dutch to sell rare national treasures, this was a case of collaboration with the enemy, and Han Van Meegeren was taken into custody. After various contradictions and denials he admitted he had sold a 'Vermeer' to Göring's agent; but then, he insisted, he had painted it himself. He was not believed. Another painting, also done by him, had even been acquired by the Boyman's Museum in Rotterdam. Experts on seventeenth-century art and two restorers from the Rijksmuseum had examined it carefully and declared it to be genuine. In an attempt to convince the experts Van Meegeren told them how he had studied Vermeer's technique for years and revealed his painting secrets. But still he was not believed. The authorities subjected his *Emmaus* picture to stringent tests and declared it to be a genuine Vermeer. Eventually he was allowed to demonstrate his skills. He chose the theme of *Christ among the Scribes*, and the experts now saw with their own eyes a 'Vermeer' materializing from the brush of Van Meegeren.

The court case was postponed for two years. Van Meegeren was not allowed to leave the country but was free to continue painting at his studio in Laren. When the case was reopened in October 1947 the court produced a list of his forgeries painted between 1937 and 1943 – seven Vermeers, among them *Christ and His Disciples in Emmaus*, completed at his studio in Nice. This had been acquired by a Dutch dealer and bought for five million guilders by the Boyman's Museum, which put it on view as one of its most valuable exhibits. On his return to Holland Van Meegeren had produced two Pieter de Hooch paintings. None of these was a copy of an existing painting.

Van Meegeren was sentenced to only a year's imprisonment because of his own confession and probably also because of the experts' embarrassed regard for him. As he was in poor health he was put in the care of the Valerius Clinic, and here, shortly after admission, he died of heart disease aged only fifty-eight.

It was Van Meegeren's daughter, Mrs Inez Randall, who explained to me that one of her father's motives for copying Vermeer's style was a resentment of critics who judge works of art without having any artistic talent themselves. His own paintings had been rejected as having little merit. When I asked Mrs Randall why he had chosen Vermeer, she explained that Vermeer had produced only fifty-two known paintings, and had apparently spent a number of uncreative years in Italy. It was this period that her father had chosen to fill. Mrs Randall also emphasized that her father never copied an existing painting, but simply adopted the artist's style and copied the signature. Curiously enough, Van Meegeren's signature and Vermeer's were similar except for the 'H' for Han and 'J' for Jan Vermeer. Art historians were aware that Vermeer had varied his signature, and it seems that but for the Goudstikker sales receipts found after the war the forgeries might never have been unmasked.

I have not been able to trace the whereabouts of Göring's fake Vermeer. Perhaps it lies forgotten in one of the depots in Munich where the less valuable of the unclaimed objects are stored.

An indication of the number of works of art passing through the main Munich collecting-point, the Führerbau (called the Gallery by the Americans), is given by the fact that in the first four months of its existence a total of 13,619 cases and uncrated works of art from thirty-eight different depositories all over Germany were recorded there. Three-quarters of this hoard came from Alt Aussee, Berchtesgaden and a monastery at Hohenfurth.

The British MFA&A unit was based in Celle, the Americans' at Wiesbaden and Munich. These experts, assisted by screened German staff and representatives of the Allied governments, spent over three years sorting out the items that poured in and having them returned to their rightful owners. Once the bulk of the looted objects had been sent back to their countries of origin the rest of the job was handed over to the Germans.

Books as well as works of art came under the jurisdiction of the art rescue teams. Since the Linz Museum was to include a large library, the ERR had been very active in confiscating collections of valuable books and manuscripts from the occupied countries. Jewish-owned collections and monastery libraries had all been carted away, ending up in monastery buildings at Tanzenberg, Carinthia, in southern Austria. There the British MFA&A teams found rooms, corridors and archways piled high with crates of valuable books from Holland, Belgium, France, Greece and even the Channel Islands. Stored here too were James de Rothschild's collection from the Château de Ferriers in France, the libraries of the cities of Kiev and Voronezh in the Soviet Union, and the Imperial Library of the Tsar of Russia. It was a formidable task sorting out the books, which totalled approximately 500,000 volumes, and then returning them to their rightful owners. Those books whose ownership could not be established were donated to the Austrian library authorities.

Restitution claims for objects confiscated from Jewish and other private sources went on for years. As late as 1963, official lists of unclaimed art objects were published in a government gazette in

Austria. And it was not until 1964 that the full story of Hitler's art looting and the Linz project was released to the world's press. Lists of missing paintings were published at the same time. A thick volume called *Verlorene Werke der Malerei* (Lost Works of Painting) was published in Munich by Ackermann Kunstverlag, giving details of the pictures missing and destroyed between 1939 and 1945 in Germany. And as late as 1973 the German Government issued an illustrated catalogue of missing works of art known to have disappeared in Italy during the Nazi period. Published in conjunction with the Italian authority for the recovery of works of art, most of it lists art treasures still missing from Florence. From my inquiries among the various international police authorities I learnt that to date (1981) none of these valuables has been recovered. Dr Siviero, in charge of the recovery of works of art in Italy, told me that there are still 1,500 items being sought, of which 1,300 are of immense artistic value. Whether these have been destroyed, are still hidden in some attic unknown to the present occupants, or have found their way through the less scrupulous dealers to private collectors in the United States, may never be known. Only recently I was told by an art expert in London that one painting which was looted is now on view in an American museum, which bought it quite legally. Unfortunately laws regarding restitution claims vary from country to country and complicate the issue.

Those works of art confiscated from German museums before the war and auctioned at Lucerne in 1939 could be regained only by purchase from their new owners, for in their case the Nazis had quite legally auctioned property belonging to the nation. No restitution claims could be made by the museums, and the Nazis had made doubly sure of this by a decree disowning any future claims. This decree, as has already been mentioned, was never rescinded by the Allies after the war. So, thanks to Hitler's pre-war policy, the greatest losses in modern art were sustained by Germany's own museums and galleries.

Just before the American forces occupied Munich the inhabitants helped themselves to the unguarded art treasures, mainly paintings, stored in the Meiserstrasse Führer depot. Although no masterpieces disappeared, a good deal of valuable stuff was carted away on barrows or in prams, and many a Munich home stored away loot that would later reappear on the black market in exchange for food or clothing. The occupying forces, frequently ignorant of art values, would exchange cartons of American cigarettes or foodstuffs for a picture they wanted to take home as a souvenir. Lost works of art do occasionally come to light. For instance, in 1964 a Monet was noticed in a German farmhouse by a visiting tourist; the farmer had taken it in exchange for a pound of butter. During a visit to the Allied Press Centre in Düsseldorf I was told the story of how one foreign correspondent had been shown by the driver of his press car four oil-paintings, each with a bullet-hole in one corner. The driver had been in the transport section of the Wehrmacht in Italy and was driving north after the evacuation of Florence's treasures when Allied aircraft attacked. He took cover. When he was able to drive on he found the truck ahead of him riddled with bullets and the driver dead. Beside the driver were four rolled-up canvases that had been penetrated by a bullet. The army driver took them back with him to Germany and held on to them after he was demobilized. When he was shown the canvases the correspondent, who was something of a connoisseur, recognized them through their covering of grime as missing church paintings from Tuscany.

Then, as far away as California, two missing Pollaiuollo paintings from Florence's Uffizi Gallery were discovered by chance in a farmhouse. It appeared that the farmer and a friend had been in the German Army and involved in the evacuation of the Uffizi works to the South Tyrol. When they were loading the trucks they took a liking to these two small pictures and decided to keep them. Some years after the war they emigrated together to Pasadena and took up farming; the pictures went with them as wartime souvenirs. By chance someone who called at the farm recognized the pictures and knew that they were on the list of missing works. The pictures are now in the Uffizi.

A detailed illustrated catalogue was published in 1963 of the missing art treasures from the Dresden Gallery. Compiled by the deputy director of the gallery, Hans Ebert, it itemized over 500 paintings known not to have been destroyed during hostilities and Allied aerial bombardments. Many of these pictures had been on loan to different Nazi local bosses and government offices in Saxony. In 1937 the Dresden Gallery owned nearly 3,000 valuable paintings, less than half of which were on display. It was not until May 1942 that the Nazi authorities consented to evacuate the invaluable collection to forty-two different depositories in castles and châteaux in Saxony out of range of Allied bombers, whose attacks on German industrial targets were increasing in intensity. In the fateful Allied air attack on Dresden in February 1945 some 200 paintings were destroyed when Dresden Castle was hit.

According to an article in the East German magazine *Sächsische Heimatblätter*, published in May 1980, the catalogue that had been circulated to the most important museum authorities around the world resulted in twenty-five paintings being recovered and returned to Dresden. Among them were paintings by Cranach the Elder, Pourbus the Elder, Jan van Goyen, and a Böcklin. Other pictures that have been identified as belonging to the Dresden Gallery were found in West Germany, Switzerland and the United States. Many legal difficulties, however, complicate their return. I was told in Vienna by the museum authorities that the Nazis had removed some paintings from museums to provinces which after the war came under Allied occupation, and in due course these were found. On the other hand, the East German authorities are reluctant to part with Austrian art treasures that fell into their hands. Negotiations to achieve an exchange arrangement satisfactory to all the parties concerned seem never ending.

Three months after their occupation of East Germany the Soviet armed forces removed 1,240 paintings to the Pushkin Museum in Moscow. Under the supervision of a woman art historian with the rank of major, Natalja Sokolowa, the damage suffered by the pictures through careless handling and storage in the aftermath of hostilities was repaired. It took ten years, by which time Khrushchev had replaced Stalin, before these pictures were returned to the Dresden Gallery. In 1958 another consignment, consisting of more paintings, as well as sculptures, graphic art and coin collections, arrived back at the Dresden Gallery from Russia.

The 1963 catalogue referred to above, lists only 400 paintings that are known to be missing. What it is unable to tell us is how many were looted and disappeared into the world's art market. At present the Dresden Gallery appears to have 2,300 of its original 3,000 paintings. What has become of the other 700, including those listed? A possible clue was the discovery of one valuable painting in the possession of a junk merchant who died in Dresden in 1974. Undoubtedly some of the other works are in East German homes or garrets.

Thus Dresden got back all the works of art that had not been destroyed by the devastating Allied air raids, and so did the Berlin museums in the eastern sector. Privately owned objects, however, were never recovered from the Soviet Union. In declassified documents at the Public Record Office, Kew, I found mentions even of British-owned objects that were never returned by the Russians occupying Lower Austria and parts of Vienna. The Russians apparently had no fine arts commissions attached to their forces, decisions on works of art being left to the discretion of individual commanders. Museums were out of bounds to Russian troops, but private property was regarded as the soldier's natural booty. Having had their own country devastated by vandals, it was not surprising that Russian soldiers took a wilful, plunderer's attitude in Germany and Austria.

The search for Europe's looted treasures goes on. Finds are still being returned to their rightful guardians or owners. Recently a Hamburg museum, checking through an inventory, discovered that they had in their storehouse an archaeological collection looted by Nazi troops from a badly damaged museum in the Crimea during the invasion of Russia. Now, in the 1980s, the collection has finally been returned to Moscow. Until quite recently Austria maintained depositories for unclaimed works of art from private ownership. These were not of great value and have now been auctioned off to the public, the profits being used for funding museum acquisitions. Today there is still a fair chance that some treasure lost from one of Europe's museums may be spotted by the trained eye at an auction sale, in an antique shop, or even tucked away in an attic.

CHAPTER THIRTEEN

The Hitler Paintings

Searching for further paintings by Hitler, I came across a reference in a book to a collection owned by the Marquess of Bath; and so it was that I visited his family home, Longleat, a magnificent Elizabethan building set in acres of Wiltshire parkland. I was taken beyond the public part of the house through a series of fine rooms into a smallish study. On the walls of this room was the Hitler collection, consisting of some sixty pictures of the dictator's own work, from his first efforts in 1906 until the end of World War I.

Lord Bath related how he came to start the collection. He happened to be at an auction at Sotheby's when two of Hitler's watercolours came up for sale. There were Jews attending the sale in order to protest against it, and when one Jewish dealer made a bid he declared that if he bought the pictures he would destroy them there and then. It was when the protesters were being ushered out that Lord Bath made his bid and gained the pictures. The vendor, a female German dealer, handed over the money from the sale to a Jewish relief organization.

Lord Bath's interest in the paintings was easy enough to explain. Since he had begun a Churchill collection, Lord Bath felt, why not a Hitler collection? Each one, in its own way, was a bit of history.

Among the Hitler watercolours at Longleat are three oil-paintings: one is of a bowl of roses, another depicts the old Ruprechtskirche in Vienna (a church in the inner city), and the third shows a view of a Lower Austrian village painted on cardboard. The last mentioned seems to have been painted around 1912, for it is of a higher standard than the earlier pictures. These three pictures appear to be the only oils Hitler painted during his Vienna period.

On the back of each picture is a letter in German authenticating its origin and the date when Hitler painted it. One of these letters stated that the painting was done while Hitler was living in the hostel for men in the Wurlitzergasse, a street in one of the outer suburbs of Vienna, and that it had then been sold to a picture framer nearby. In all my research I had not come across this address before, nor had the street name been mentioned in any of the biographies of Hitler. Some of these maintain that he had slept rough for a time, but all agree that the only hostel he had lived in was the one in the Meldemannstrasse, newly built in 1906 at the bequest of Emperor Franz Josef I as a home for bachelors of low income. In reply to my inquiries, the Vienna municipal authorities confirmed that there had been a hostel in the Wurlitzergasse, pulled down a few years earlier, though they had no evidence of Hitler's having stayed there. It was only on my last visit to Vienna that I was able to contact the writer of the letters authenticating the pictures: a Herr Peter Jahn, himself an art dealer, who today is the only living expert on Hitler's paintings. He received me in his beautifully furnished flat in one of Vienna's residential quarters, and told me the background story of the Hitler paintings he had acquired over the years.

Before Austria was annexed by Hitler in 1937, Herr Jahn was approached by the German art expert, Herr Schulte Stratthaus, who was attached to the German Embassy in Vienna. Stratthaus had been appointed by Hitler to buy up any privately owned paintings by him in Austria that he could find. Jahn had been chosen because he had been a consultant during the furnishing of the embassy and had the right connections among art dealers. He continued the job of rounding up Hitler pictures until his army call-up during the war.

The discovery of the Van Eyck altar-piece, looted from Ghent, at Alt Ausee salt-mine.

The Ghent altar-piece after being removed from a mineshaft.

Soldiers of the US 7th Army removing pictures found at Neuschwanstein
Castle, Fussen, near the Swiss border.

MFA&A (Monuments, Fine Arts and Archives) officers inspecting treasures looted from Polish churches, found in Grasleben salt-mine.

Part of Göring's collection, assembled in a house in Berchtesgaden. Among the pictures are three Rembrandts, three Cranachs and a fifteenth-century statue of Eve.

US fine arts officers with Vermeer's *The Artist in His Studio*. The picture was acquired by Hitler from Count Czernin shortly after the annexation of Austria. Like many of the works of art destined for the Linz Museum, it was discovered in the salt-mines at Alt Aussee.

The Artist in His Studio by Vermeer. Following
restitution disputes, it now hangs in the
Kunsthistorisches Museum, Vienna.

Jan Wildens by Van Dyck; another painting missing from the
Kunsthistorisches Museum which is known not to have been destroyed and
is still being sought.

Ecce Homo by Antonello da Messina, one of the paintings missing from the Kunsthistorisches Museum but believed to be still in existence somewhere.

Bundles of forged £5 notes being brought ashore at Lake Töplitz in 1959. Millions of pounds' worth of counterfeit currency was dumped in wooden boxes into the lake during the last days of the war.

The main railway station at Linz today.

Hitler surveys his model for the rebuilding of Linz. This photograph was taken in his Berlin bunker shortly before he committed suicide.

When Hitler came to power many of his watercolours had turned up for sale in Germany, for the Nazi leaders were naturally keen to own a picture by the Führer. As a result a number of fakes were painted and put on the market in several countries. A former friend of Hitler's from the Meldemannstrasse days, Hanisch, who had hawked Hitler's pictures around the city, decided to cash in on this situation. As was mentioned earlier, Hanisch had parted company with Hitler in Vienna (in 1909) when Hitler accused him of embezzling the money from the sale of a watercolour of the Reichsrat, with the result that Hanisch spent a few days in jail. Hanisch was something of an artist himself, and twenty-five years after this incident he decided to use his knowledge of Hitler's style to gain his revenge. He had no difficulty in producing views of Vienna in Hitler's simple style. To give them an authentic look he put them in a warm oven that turned the paper a brownish colour. He charged modest prices, sold the pictures abroad, and the business thrived until Hitler annexed Austria. Then the Gestapo caught up with Hanisch, whereupon he was arrested and, soon after, Herr Jahn affirmed, died mysteriously in a Vienna prison. He knew too much. Hanisch had also published a book about his time with Hitler, most of which is regarded by serious biographers as very unreliable.

To be able to distinguish the genuine Hitler paintings from the fakes, Jahn needed more background information. He had two private interviews with Hitler in the Braune Haus, headquarters of the Nazi Party in Munich. Hitler confirmed that he had lived in the men's hostel in the Wurlitzergasse before moving to the Meldemannstrasse hostel, where he turned out a large number of watercolour reproductions of postcards and old prints of Vienna. Hitler estimated that in his six years of artistic work in Vienna and Munich, from 1908 to 1914, he produced over a thousand paintings, a few of them in oils. He also told Herr Jahn that he painted simply to earn a living and never regarded himself as an artist; his natural bent was for architectural design. This is apparent in the detail Hitler gives to the buildings in his pictures – especially noticeable, according to Herr Jahn, in Hitler's watercolour of the Gloriette summerhouse in the gardens of the palace at Schönbrunn, summer seat of the Austrian emperors. Hitler painted it while he was living in the Wurlitzergasse and sold it to a picture-framer in a nearby street. It was common practice at the time to offset a frame that was in the window for sale by putting a pleasant landscape picture inside it, and this particular one was used over and over again. It had remained with the picture-framer's family until discovered by Herr Jahn.

When in 1964 I myself was trying to trace Hitler's paintings I came across an elderly couple who showed me their oak bedstead, the head of which was decorated with a rather amateurish landscape. The young artist responsible for this, they recalled, was none other than Adolf Hitler. It was common practice in middle-class Viennese homes before World War I to have furniture and upright pianos decorated in this way.

I asked Herr Jahn about one particular watercolour in Lord Bath's collection, a house in a landscape, surrounded by a decoration of flowers. On the reverse of this picture is a dedication to an innkeeper, Herr Jaegerhofer, and his wife. Herr Jahn had ascertained that this man was the owner of a small restaurant where Hitler took some of his meals when he was living in the Stumpergasse.

I had noticed one picture in the Longleat collection which seemed to be of a better standard than the others, a view of the Karlskirche, a domed church in Vienna. Such church views were much favoured by Hitler, Herr Jahn told me, because they were particularly easy to sell. Hitler had varied his painting techniques, he said, sometimes adopting the style of a miniaturist, but he had never failed to strive for architectural accuracy. Had he taken the advice of the Rector of the Academy of Fine Arts in his youth and studied architecture he might have been reasonably successful. He was even commissioned once to prepare designs for a villa in Vienna, though it was never built. After World War I he concentrated especially on architectural design, and in 1925 made all the sketches for the new Linz – though he had not yet visualized it as an art centre.

Hitler admitted to Herr Jahn that he could not draw figures. One particular watercolour, *Courtyard in a Viennese Biedermeier House*, reproduced from an old print, has three very crudely sketched figures in it. This appears to have been one of his earlier efforts. Herr Jahn said he had never come across such distorted figures in a painting before.

Hitler's first known attempt at a painting to survive, dated 1906 and now in the Longleat collection, shows a small village with a church. On the reverse, in Hitler's own handwriting, is this dedication: 'In memory. Your Adolf Hitler.' To whom it was addressed is unknown, but this must have been one of the pictures he showed his friend August Kubizek, who found them lifeless and uninteresting. The motif of the church spire cannot have been used purely for reasons of saleability, since, as Herr Jahn pointed out to me, Hitler was fascinated by this particular feature and frequently introduced a spire into his pictures.

From the time Herr Jahn started his search for Hitler's pictures in 1937 up to the time of our talk, he had, he said, visited and spoken to most of the Vienna picture-framers – many of them since dead – who Hitler had dealt with. One of these, who had the Jewish name of Morgenstern, and most of whose customers were Jewish, remembered well the shabbily dressed young man who brought his commissioned landscapes round punctually every week. Six of these landscapes were discovered by Herr Jahn in Vienna as late as 1968. They had been inherited by a woman whose mother-in-law had originally bought them from Morgenstern.

Hitler's painting output seems to have been quite considerable. If, as Herr Jahn said, he churned out over a thousand works between 1908 and 1914, he must have done about three paintings a week, which does seem to disprove the assumption of some biographers that as an adult he was too lazy to work unless forced to do so. This large output seems to fall into two groups: the mass-produced views which he could easily sell as souvenirs, and the pictures on which he spent some time and effort. A good example of the latter is the one known oil-painting he did of a vase of flowers.

Apparently in his more expansive and generous moods Hitler would present his favourites with paintings from among those he had kept for himself. Göring, Himmler and even Mussolini were favoured in this way. A mystery still surrounds some twenty Hitler paintings which were believed to be in Mussolini's possession and which turned up again after World War II in Rome, only to vanish again, believed to have been stolen.

During Hitler's lifetime his signed paintings were fetching very high prices, until the demand in Germany suddenly slumped and their value dropped. According to Herr Jahn, Hitler was attending a reception given for him in a wealthy industrialist's home when the hostess proudly showed him one of his paintings that she owned. When she told him that she had paid several thousand Reichsmarks for it he was enraged. Such a sum, he said, would once have paid for him to take a complete architectural course. He was disgusted to think that people were profiteering from the work for which he had been paid a mere pittance. The story got around, and as a result prominent Nazis, some of whom had regarded his pictures as an investment, stopped buying them.

This may have been why Hitler ordered Schulte Stratthaus and others to buy up any of his paintings they could find to be stored away in the Braune Haus archives. They were specially anxious to find the three pictures Hitler had submitted for his Academy entrance examination, which he sold after the Academy returned them to him. They were traced, but the owner refused to sell, though he loaned the pictures to the Vienna Nazi Party Gauhaus. In the aftermath of the war they disappeared from there, and it was not until the 1960s that Herr Jahn managed to uncover them in the possession of relatives of the former owner. Now they are in the collection at Longleat, Lord Bath having acquired them from him.

I learnt that Hitler's Jewish family doctor, Dr Bloch, owned some of the Hitler paintings. Hitler had given them to him as a young man, in gratitude for having looked after his ailing mother so well. On the day Hitler marched into Linz with his forces, Gestapo agents started an intensive search for the documents relating to Hitler's call-up in 1913 which he tried to evade, and also visited Dr Bloch's surgery. They were looking for those early pictures, which Bloch had kept in the hope that they would save him from persecution. The Gestapo thugs found them, took them away, and sealed off Bloch's flat. Bloch's daughter then visited the Gestapo offices to ask what further action would be taken. None, they assured her; they had found what they wanted and Dr Bloch could continue his practice, treating Jewish patients only. Indeed, if he wished, he would be allowed to emigrate; the choice was his. She and her husband took advantage of this offer and went to America. Dr Bloch himself stayed on for some time, unmolested by the Nazi authorities, and then a couple of years later he joined his daughter in New York. His account of his relations with the young Adolf and his family was published in the American press. He died in the United States.

The improvement in the architectural detail in the Hitler pictures is visible from around the time he moved to Munich in 1913. Again he concentrated on popular views like that of the old town hall, where all civil weddings took place; very saleable as a souvenir, and painted so many times by Hitler that he could do it from memory. He also painted the Bürgerbräu, the famous Munich beer-cellar, little realizing that one day it would be the Nazi Party meeting-place and political platform and that an attempt on his life would be made there. In 1913, just as it is today, the strong frothy beer would have been served in 2-litre glasses by buxom waitresses, and Hitler would have joined the crowd like any other Munich citizen or tourist. In the Munich days he received a steady stream of commissions, and painted landscapes as well as town views, one of his favourites being the Königsee in Bavaria.

The 1914–18 war provided a quite different background for Hitler's painting. For one thing, once in the army he was drawing from nature. As Herr Jahn pointed out to me, the work he did then shows a change for the better. An ink-and-wash drawing dated 1914, entitled *Trench at Douaumont*, provides evidence of this improvement. Hitler must have kept this picture for some time after the war, as there is a dedication on the reverse to a Herr Tschammer Osten dated 1926. The picture then came into the possession of the former Austrian ambassador to Rome, Rintelen, who became one of the leading Nazis after the annexation of his country. His widow later sold the picture to a Viennese art dealer and it was purchased by a private collector. Herr Jahn bought it in 1966, and it finally ended up at Longleat. Hitler produced a number of watercolours painted in the front line during these early years. He also designed menu cards for the officers' mess.

The Führer's paintings continue to come up for sale, and in the United States collectors pay high prices for them. There are even a few in museums.

When I visited Herr Jahn a second time he showed me three watercolours that had been sent to him for his opinion. One was rather unusual – the interior of a church, but without any human figures. The other two were of ruined buildings at the front in World War I. The signature – A.H. or A. Hitler – is easily faked, but often the paper or cardboard gives Herr Jahn a clue about the picture's authenticity. Herr Jahn explained to me that when the young Hitler was short of cash he would often paint on the back of any discarded drawing-paper he could get hold of. An example is his picture of the church at Pötzleinsdorf, a garden suburb below the slopes of the Vienna Woods. On the reverse of this there are some technical sketches signed by a Kurt Mayer – no doubt a student who gave Hitler the paper when he had finished with it.

In 1980 a picture by Hitler, described as uninspired and drab, was sold by auction in a Cornwall saleroom for £320 to an Italian dealer. It had been discovered by a Lancashire collector of military paintings in a lot he bought at a flea market in England. Such a picture, if genuine, would have fetched a few thousand dollars in the United States where, according to Herr Jahn, there is considerable demand for them. But many a proud owner probably possesses a fake. It is not surprising that Herr Jahn is often summoned to America by collectors and paid well for his expertise – though even that is not infallible.

As to Hitler's real talent, opinions about it vary. Certainly he had distinct architectural ability, as Speer and others recognized when they saw his plans for Linz and other cities, some of which in fact materialized and survived World War II. But in Vienna I was told that, when a few years ago one of the teachers at the Vienna Academy of Fine Arts was asked his opinion of an un-signed watercolour, he said that if it had been done by someone under fifteen it showed some talent, but if by anyone over that age it was distinctly amateurish. The picture was painted by Hitler in 1910, when he was twenty-one. On the other hand, Professor Werner Maser, the eminent German historian and expert on the Hitler era, has written that many a famous artist has left us far worse pictures from his early days than Hitler did.

Epilogue

Over forty years have passed since Hitler first planned his great art centre at Linz. Why was it that with all the resources at his disposal Hitler progressed no further than building the Nibelungen Bridge that today links the old town with the suburb of Urfahr?

When I revisited Linz I was able to meet the now retired chief engineer who was appointed by Hitler to supervise the construction of the bridge. He told me that Hitler's original idea was to erect a very high suspension bridge, but in 1940 there were no German steelworks capable of forging cast-iron chains strong enough to carry the weight that would have to be borne. New plans were submitted, and Hitler was eventually forced to agree to the austere-looking version that survives. It was finished, as ordered, in two years. However, when the four outsize symbolic figures of the Nibelungen Saga were put in place on the completed structure for Hitler's inspection, the engineers noticed that the entire perspective of the bridge looking towards the old town appeared out of alignment.

Why were none of the other planned buildings ever built? In answer to this question I was told that while the overall supervision had at first been in the hands of Albert Speer, his other commitments had taken up too much of his time for him to give much attention to Linz. Consequently Hitler appointed as Reichsrat (an honorary title conferred by the Führer, equivalent to Federal Councillor) Roderick Fick, a great admirer of his and a former boat-builder turned architect. Fick was to design and build the great Linz art centre. Hitler was pleased by the plans Fick had based on Hitler's sketches; but apparently Fick was a rather conceited man who could not get on with his colleagues. Eventually Hitler realized he was not capable of carrying out the work, and he was relegated to building blocks of flats on the outskirts of Linz. Professor Hermann Giesler was then appointed. He was already in charge of rebuilding in Munich, including the Nazi headquarters and the adjoining mausoleum for Hitler.

Throughout the war Hitler frequented Giesler's Munich studio, where a large-scale model of the new Linz project was being constructed. He would discuss new ideas with Giesler and suggest possible improvements. It was not until February 1945 that the model was completed and installed by Giesler in an underground room of the Reichskanzlei in Berlin, adjoining Hitler's military headquarters in the bunker. Daily Hitler would brood over this model of Linz. A specially designed lighting system enabled him to manipulate spotlights to create the effects of sunshine at different times of the day and year so that he could see where the shadows fell. Often after discussing the latest military situation with his generals he would usher them in to look at the model and tell them of his grandiose plans for the town. When Kaltenbrunner found himself listening to all this even while the Russian shells were pounding the devastated city, he felt he was in the company of a madman obsessed with his model toy. To the end, as the Third Reich collapsed around him, Hitler would spend time every day poring over the model.

I discovered photographs of the model in the archives of the Linz Landesmuseum in 1965, but I could not ascertain what had become of the actual model. Only recently I learnt through correspondence with Professor Giesler, now retired and living in Germany, that it had been removed from the Berlin bunker in March 1945 and taken to a depository in Bavaria. There it must have been destroyed in the aftermath of the war. The only part of the model to be realized in actual construction was the bridge which is still standing.

I found out what the Linz Museum would have contained from a small pamphlet shown to me by Dr Kugler, superintendent of the library at the Kunsthistorisches Museum in Vienna. This was published by Heinrich Hoffmann, in honour of Hitler's birthday on 20th April, 1945, and intended for distribution among the armed forces. The frontispiece is a reproduction in colour of the famous Vermeer painting *The Artist in His Studio*, acquired under pressure in 1938 from the Czernin collection in Vienna. The anonymous author of the pamphlet describes the plans for the gallery. It was to contain a limited selection of fine European art, but in particular, thanks to the Führer's purchases, it was to be a centre for Germanic art. What others had taken centuries to create, one man, because of his devotion to the arts and refusal to be daunted, had been creating single-handed. In the 1930s great national treasures were lost by sales abroad, until the Führer put a stop to this shameful traffic. As an example the writer cites Vermeer's *The Artist in His Studio* which was nearly sold to the United States for $6 million.

The pamphlet lists various paintings to be exhibited in the new Linz gallery. There is a colour reproduction of *The Plague in Florence*, by the Austrian painter Hans Makart, which Mussolini had given to Hitler. I noticed also *The Hay Harvest* by Pieter Brueghel the Elder, which had been the property of the princely Lobkowitz family and was looted from their castle, Raudnitz, in Czechoslovakia. It is referred to as 'a new acquisition'. Each of the gallery's rooms was to be decorated and furnished in the style of the period of the paintings, the pamphlet explains. There would be a small gallery just for Makart, and one for Rudolf von Alt together with selected furnishings of his period. The Linz gallery was to become a centre for the art of the past, just as the Haus der Deutschen Kunst in Munich, also created by Hitler, was a centre for German contemporary art. The remainder of the pamphlet gives a lyrical description, illustrated with watercolours, of Hitler's birthplace of Braunau, on the Inn River, and the neighbouring village of Lambach where he went to school. It seems doubtful that this tribute to the Führer's contributions to the world of art achieved a wide distribution, appearing as it did just a few weeks before Nazi Germany's capitulation. It must have had Hitler's approval, but who ordered its publication? Was it a last-minute propaganda effort by Goebbels to boost morale in a defeated army? Only the publisher, Hoffmann, could have provided the answer, and he is dead.

Today's citizens of Linz are unaware of Hitler's plans for rebuilding their city. Indeed it is lucky that it never materialized, for it would have ruined the atmosphere of the old quarter. Postwar planners have introduced pedestrian precincts and shopping centres, and in the park beside the Danube stands Austria's most modern concert hall, dedicated to Bruckner, the great Linz composer. On the Freinberg, where the young Hitler once sketched his visions of a new Linz, there is now a vast sports stadium overlooking the town. Modern tower blocks have sprung up on the Urfahr side of the river where Hitler lived with his mother. Gone is the old interior of the theatre with its alcoves and gilded columns, where Hitler witnessed that fateful performance of *Rienzi*. The musty atmosphere that I remember from 1965 has been replaced by a modern auditorium with comfortable seating. During the last two decades Linz has had an impressive face-lift which has made it a bustling and lively place and a centre for music. Recently the Linz Museum director wanted to exhibit the photographs and plans of Hitler's project which would have defaced the historic old town, but the city councillors objected. Yet I was told by the town's tourist director that many foreign tourists, especially Americans, come to Linz specifically to see the place where Hitler had spent some of his youth.

That Hitler's failure as architect and artist may have been a driving motive behind his rise to power was confirmed for me by a German doctor I spoke to and also by Robert Waite, Professor of History at Williams College in Williamstown, Massachusetts, and author of *The Psychopathic God: Adolf Hitler*. In this book Waite makes a detailed analysis of Hitler's demoniacal personality. He confirmed to me that in his view there was a direct association in Hitler's mind between being an artist and being a creative and innovative political leader. The compulsions to destroy and rebuild were deeply rooted in Hitler – though he succeeded only in the former activity. Even on his fifty-sixth – and last – birthday, in April 1945, he was working obsessively until the early hours of the morning on his plans for Linz. He lived in a world of fantasy, hate and fire. He liked to compare himself to Napoleon, though he does not seem to have learnt from Bonaparte's military disasters. His plans for buildings, Speer has commented, suggested coldness and impersonality, the very expression of tyranny. Often during his life he contemplated suicide, and at these times he would remark to his entourage that the world would lose a great artist in him. But when Hjalmar Schacht, Germany's wartime financial wizard, was interrogated after the war, he maintained that in fact Hitler was half-educated and never learnt much from his wide reading. Rightly he called himself Europe's greatest actor and he was well aware that his gifts were essentially diabolic. He was not simply immoral, in Schacht's opinion, but quite amoral.

Could European history have taken quite another turn if Hitler had not been rejected by the Academy of Fine Arts in Vienna? Or, in the absence of Hitler, would some other political agitator have come to the fore and set himself the task of driving the German nation into a political frenzy? We shall never know the answers to these questions. All we can say with any certainty is that if Hitler had settled into a career as an architect or artist, at least the art treasures of centuries, and of a whole continent, might not have been ravaged.

APPENDIX

Sources of Information on Missing Works of Art

A detailed list of all the valuable paintings from Germany's museums and art galleries which were either destroyed or stolen between 1939 and 1945, or as a consequence of the war, was published in a large volume *Verlorene Werke der Malerei* (Lost Paintings) by the Friedrich Adolf Ackermanns Kunstverlag in Munich in 1965. This book is recognized by museum authorities as a standard work on missing paintings believed still to be in existence but whose whereabouts are unknown. The following is a selection of the many paintings that are still being sought:

CANALETTO, Giovanni Antonio (1697–1768), *Ansicht des Dogenpalastes von Venedig* (View of the Doge's Palace in Venice). Oil on canvas. 72×95 cm.

CARAVAGGIO, Il (Michelangelo Merisi) (1569–1609), *Grablegung Christi* (Internment of Christ). Oil on canvas. 157×107 cm. (looted)

CÉZANNE, Paul (1839–1905), *Landschaft von Auvers sur Oise* (landscape). Oil on canvas. 48×58 cm.

CORINTH, Lovis (1858–1925), *Pietà*. Oil on canvas. 128·5×160 cm.

COURBET, Gustave (1819–1877), *Landschaft bei Ornans* (Landscape near Ornans). Oil on canvas. 57×71·5 cm.

CRANACH, Lucas (1472–1553), *Lukretia*. Oil on wood. 57×38 cm.

DOMENICHINO, Il (Domenico Zampieri) (1581–1641), *Der Hl Hieronymus* (St Hieronymus). Oil on canvas. 58·5×41·5 cm.

DÜRER, Albrecht (1471–1528), *Salvator Mundi* (Christ's Head). Oil on wood. 21×18 cm.

——, *Bildniss Felicitas Tucher* (Portrait of Felicitas Tucher) (Diptychon). Oil on wood.

FRIEDRICH, Caspar David (1774–1840), *Landschaft mit Regenbogen* (Landscape with Rainbow). Oil on canvas. 59×84·5 cm.

GIORDANO, Luca (1634–1705), *St Jacob von Compostella*. Oil on canvas. 125×79 cm.

HALS, Frans (1580?–1666), *Brustbild eines Manner* (Torso of a Man). Oil on canvas. 87×82 cm.

HUYSMANS, Jan Baptist (1654–1716), *Reste eines Korinthischen Temples* (Ruins of a Corinthian Temple). 54·5×94 cm. (looted)

LOCATELLI, Andrea (d. *c.* 1741), *Landschaft bei Sonnenaufgang* (Landscape with Sunrise). 45×35 cm. (looted)

MONET, Claude (1840–1926), *Der Park* (The Park). Oil on canvas. 75×100 cm.

NANI, Giacomo (1701–1770), *Blumenstrausse* (Bunch of Flowers). Oil on canvas. 87×63 cm.

PANNINI, Giovanni Paolo (*c.* 1692–1765), *Architekturbild* (Architectural). Canvas. 44×34 cm.

RENOIR, Auguste (1841–1919), *Dame am Fenster* (Madame Choquet) (Lady at Window). Oil on canvas. 67×54 cm.

REYNOLDS, Sir Joshua (1723–1792), *Mädchen mi Blumen* (Girl with Flowers). Oil on canvas. 77×55·5 cm. (stolen)

STEEN, Jan (*c.* 1626–1679), *Lustige Gesellschaft in einer Schenke* (Jolly Crowd in an Inn). Oil on wood. 48×36 cm.

STUCK, Franz von (1863–1928), *Salome*. Oil on wood. 105×93 cm.

TENIERS, David (1582–1649), *Wirhtshausstube* (Inn Room). Oil on canvas. 15×21 cm.

VAN DYCK, Sir Anthony (1599–1641), *Die Speisung der Fümftausend* (Feeding of the Five Thousand). Oil on canvas. 157×228 cm.

VAN GOYEN, Jan (1596–1656), *Am Kornfeld* (Cornfield). Oil on wood. Circular 12 cm.

VAUTIER, Benjamin (1829–1898), *Der Gang zum Standesamt* (The Walk to the Registry Office). Oil on canvas. 40×58 cm.

VERMEER, Jan (1632–1675), *Baumgruppe mit Lagernder Family und Reitergruppe* (Trees with Resting Family and Horse Riders). 54×44 cm.

WITHERS, Alfred (1856–1932), *Die Mühle* (The Mill). Canvas. 54×71 cm.

Even greater is the number of prominent German nineteenth-century painters whose pictures are known to have been looted or that disappeared from their wartime depots. Many of these are believed to be in private possession.

Italy, which is still searching for over 1,300 valuable art treasures, has in conjunction with the German authorities printed a booklet listing the works of art known to have been taken by the Nazis from their country. Florentine works figure prominently among these, of which the following is a small selection:

ANON., c. 1583, *The Martyrdom of the Forty Saints Martyrs.* Panel, with a gilt frame. 24×17 cm. Finaly collection, Florence.

BELLA, Stefano della (1610–1644), *View of Sant' Angelo Castle.* Pen drawing. 15×30 cm. Uffizi Gallery, Florence.

BELLOTTO, Bernardo (1720–1780), *The Grand Canal in Venice.* Canvas. 84×58 cm. Borbone-Parma collection.

BIONDO, Giovanni del (1356–1392), *The Annunciation.* Panel. Each wing 13×27 cm. Uffizi Gallery, Florence.

BRANDIMARTE, Benedetto (1588–1592), *The Madonna with Child and Two Saints* (on the back *Madonna with Child* and small study of a nude). Pen and white lead drawing. 35×29 cm. Finaly collection, Florence. (Active for four years.)

BRONZINO, Angelo (1503–1572) (school of), *Francesco de' Medici.* Canvas. 103×143·5 cm frame. National Gallery, Rome. In deposit with the FF. AA. Officers Club at the Barberìni Palace, Rome.

—— (manner of), *Portrait of a Girl.* 24×18 cm. Uffizi Gallery, Florence.

CALLOT, Jacques (1593–1635), *Temptation of St Anthony.* Pen and bistre on paper. 47×75 cm. Uffizi Gallery, Florence, Department of Drawings and Prints.

CAMBIASO, Luca (1527–1585), *Battle: God the Father and Angels in the High Sky.* Pen and aquatint drawing. 59×83 cm. Finaly collection, Florence.

CANALETTO, Giovanni Antonio (1697–1768), *The Schiavoni Riva towards the East.* Canvas. 80×58 cm. Borbone-Parma collection.

CARDI, Ludovico (called il Cigoli) (1559–1613), *The Martyrdom of St Stephen*. Watercolour and white lead on coloured paper. 114×84 cm. Uffizi Gallery, Florence, Department of Drawings and Prints.

CELLINI, Benvenuto (manner of) (1500–1571), Oval plate. Gilt silver with embossed figures. 64×53 cm; weight 4390 kg. Museo degli Argenti, Pitti Palace, Florence, coming from the Medici collection.

CHARDIN, J. B. (1699–1779), *Sitting Woman* (profile). Canvas. *c*. 30×40 cm. Property of Mrs Giulia Radicati Guadagni, Naples.

CLOUET, François (d. 1572), *Feminine Portrait*. Panel. 28×18 cm. Finaly collection, Florence.

COURTOIS, Jac. (called il Borgognone) (1621–1675), manner of, *Battle*. Canvas. 32×50 cm. Uffizi Gallery, Florence. In deposit at the Villa Cisterna, Via della Pietra.

DOSIO, Giovanni Antonio (1533–1609), *Ancient Façade of St Peter* with view of the Michelangelo tambour (drum). Pen and watercolour drawing. 27×27 cm. Uffizi Gallery, Florence, Department of Drawings and Prints.

——, *View of the Borgo Alessandrino in Rome*. Pen and watercolour drawing. 20×33 cm. Uffizi Gallery, Florence, Department of Drawings and Prints.

FERRETTI, Gian Domenico (1692–*c*. 1768), *Sacrifice of Abraham*. Canvas. 61×90 cm. Uffizi Gallery, Florence.

FLORENTINE SCHOOL, sixteenth century, *Portrait of Unknown Woman*. Canvas. 32×23 cm. Uffizi Gallery, Florence. In deposit at the warehouse of the Via Lambertesca, later in the Occhi deposit at the Pitti Palace; then in the Borgo deposit in Buggiano.

FRAGONARD, Jean Honoré (1732–1806), *Three Men and a Boy beneath a Sacrificial Altar*. Drawing, signed, in gilt frame. Finaly collection, Florence.

GRAZIANI, Francesco (called Ciccio Napoletano) (active in the seventeenth century), *Cavalry Battle*. 22×32 cm. Uffizi Gallery, Florence.

ITALIAN SCHOOL, eighteenth century, *Landscape with Hunters*. Canvas. 52×82 cm. Uffizi Gallery, Florence.

——, *Seaport*. Painting on canvas. Uffizi Gallery, Florence.

——, *Sea View with Ruins*. Painting on canvas. 42×55 cm. Uffizi Gallery, Florence.

LIGOZZI, Jacopo (*c.* 1547–1626), *Bombardier*. Uffizi Gallery, Florence.

MEHUS, Livio (1630–1691), *Seaport*. Canvas. 63×99 cm. Uffizi Gallery, Florence.

MEMLING, Hans (1433–1494), *Portrait of a Young Man*. Panel. 35×24 cm. Uffizi Gallery, Florence.

MEULEN, Adam F. van der (1634–1690), *Passage of Louis XIV over the Rhine*. Canvas. Borbone-Parma collection.

MICHELANGELO BUONARROTI (1475–1564), *Mask of a Faun*. Sculpture in marble. National Museum, Florence.

MONALDI, Carlo (1690–1760), *Men at Table*. 25×37 cm. Uffizi Gallery, Florence.

NALDINI, Battista (1537–1591), *The Deposition* (at the back are two standing figures). Pen drawing. 13×15 cm. Finaly collection, Florence.

——, *The Deposition*. Pen and sepia drawing, round. Diameter 15 cm. Finaly collection, Florence.

ONOFRI, Crescenzio (1632–1698), *Landscape*. Canvas. 99×123 cm. Uffizi Gallery, Florence.

PARMIGIANINO (1503–1540), *Sacred Family*. Pencil drawing, oval. 6·5×5·5 cm. Finaly collection, Florence.

—— (school of), sixteenth century, *Madonna with Child and the Infant St John*. Oil on panel. 33×25 cm. Gilt and carved frame. Finaly collection, Florence.

PASSAROTTI, Bartolomeo (1529–1592), *Moses on the Hill*. Pen drawing. 25×19 cm. Finaly collection, Florence.

——, *Study of a Left Foot*. Pen drawing. 20×12 cm. Finaly collection, Florence.

PITATI, Bonifacio de' (1487–1553), *Farinata Degli Uberti*. Canvas. 47×62 cm (with frame, 59×70 cm). National Gallery, Rome. In deposit with the FF. AA. Officers Club at the Barberini Palace, Rome.

——, *Philippus Scolarius*. Canvas. 49×66 cm (with frame, 65×81 cm). National Gallery, Rome. In deposit with the FF. AA. Officers Club at the Barberini Palace, Rome.

——, *Sciarra Colonna*. Canvas. 47×62 cm (with frame, 59×74 cm). National Gallery, Rome. In deposit with the FF. AA. Officers Club at the Barberini Palace, Rome.

PIOMBO, Sebastiano del (1485–1547), *Portrait of the Cardinal Ippolito de' Medici*. Museo di Palazzo Venezia, Rome. In deposit from 1941 care of the Museo della Torre di Pandolfo Capodiferro, Minturno.

POUSSIN, Nicolas (1594–1665), *Group of Standing Men and Women with Children in Their Arms*. Sepia drawing. 17×32 cm. Finaly collection, Florence.

RAPHAEL (1483–1520), *Madonna of the Veil*. Black pencil and chalk on yellow paper. 77×73 cm. Uffizi Gallery, Florence.

REMBRANDT VAN RIJN (1606–1669), *Self-portrait*. Panel. Renaissance frame gilt and painted. 37×33 cm. Finaly collection, Florence.

RODOLFO, Michele di (attributed to) (1503–1577), *The Archangel and Tobiah*. 99×49 cm. Uffizi Gallery, Florence (attributed to F. Grabacci).

ROSA, Salvator (1615–1673), *Battle*. Panel. 10×23 cm. Uffizi Gallery, Florence. In deposit at the Villa Cisterna, Via della Pietra.

RUBENS, Peter Paul (1577–1640), *Virtue*. Painting representing three feminine figures, three 'putti' and a dove. Rome, private collection.

SALIMBENI, Arcangelo (1530/40–after 1580), *The Madonna of the Misericord*. Sepia drawing. 16×23 cm. Finaly collection, Florence.

——, *St Mary Magdalen*. Red chalk. 26×22 cm. Finaly collection, Florence.

——, *The Time Smashed by a Rock*. Drawing. 16×23 cm. Finaly collection, Florence.

SALVIATI, Francesco (1510–1563), *The Deposition*. Pen drawing. 26×20 cm. Finaly collection, Florence.

'strocchi' collection of historical, classical stringed musical instruments (sixteenth, seventeenth and eighteenth centuries). The pieces, protected by paper, were placed in large boxes. Each one had two labels, one blue and one sepia coloured, with the name of the maker or the attribution, the historical period and, in red, the price at the time when they were purchased.

STROZZI, Bernardo (1581–1644), *Deposition*. Pen and sepia drawing. 28×21 cm. Finaly collection, Florence.

TEMPESTA, Antonio (1555–1630), *St Sebastian and Another Saint in Glory*. Pen drawing. 14×14 cm. Finaly collection, Florence.

TINTORETTO, Jacapo (1518–1594), *Jesus Dead Supported by Two Angels*. Red chalk. 28×69 cm. Uffizi Gallery, Florence, Department of Drawings and Prints.

TITIAN (1490–1576) (school of), *Venus*. Canvas. (Solicitor) Gino Pincherle collection.

TOSCHI, Pier Francesco di Jacopo (1502–1567), *The Magi Kings*. Panel. The composition is enclosed in a cartiglio, part of predella. 16×39 cm. Uffizi Gallery, Florence.

UNKNOWN from seventeenth century, *Landscape*. Canvas. 58×71 cm. Uffizi Gallery, Florence.

VANNI, Francesco (1563–1610), *Madonna with Child and St Francis*. Red chalk drawing. 26×19 cm. Finaly collection, Florence.

—— (attributed to), *An Old Man Offers a Crown to a Youth*. Pen drawing. 15×12 cm. Finaly collection, Florence.

—— (1563–1610), *Woman and Warrior in a Wood*. Sepia drawing. 20×14 cm. Finaly collection, Florence.

VENETIAN SCHOOL, sixteenth century, *Masculine Portrait*. Canvas. 54×41 cm. Uffizi Gallery, Florence.

VERONESE, Paolo (1528–1588) (school of). *Adoration of the Magi*. Canvas. 145×145? cm. Uffizi Gallery, Florence. In deposit at the Villa Cisterna, Via della Pietra.

ZUCCARI, Federico (1540–1609), *Man and Woman inside an Architectural Frame*. Pen, bistre and red pencil drawing. 18×15 cm. Finaly collection, Florence.

In Austria the Kunsthistorisches Museum in Vienna lists a number of Gobelin tapestries which were loaned by Göring for Karinhall. These have not been recovered, nor have a number of paintings (of which two are reproduced on pages 158 and 159). Nazi-confiscated Jewish-owned works of art found in depots and earmarked for Linz were returned to their rightful owners. But much has never been recovered. In one particular instance five valuable paintings belonging to Mrs Madeleine Duke are still being sought, believed to be in Germany. These are: Botticelli's *Florentine Lady*, Canaletto's *Santa Maria della Salute and Grand Canal*, Lucas Cranach's *Adam and Eve in Paradise*, a Rembrandt *Self-portrait* and Vermeyen's *Portrait of Maximillian I*.

Bibliography

Best, Karl, *Die Verwaltung in Polen*. Berlin, 1940.

Binion, Rudolf, *Hitler among Germans*. Oxford: Elsevier, 1976.

Boldt, Gerhard, *Die Letzten Tage*. Zürich, 1947.

Bormann, Martin, *Bormann's Letters*. London: Weidenfeld & Nicolson, 1954.

Bouhler, Philip, *Adolf Hitler*. Berlin: Terramare Office, 1938.

Branscombe, Peter (Ed.), *Austrian Life and Literature 1780–1938: Eight Essays*. Edinburgh: Scottish Academic Press, 1978.

Brenner, Hildegard, *Kunstpolitik des National Sozialismus*. Hamburg: Rowohlt Taschenbuch Verlag, 1963.

Bunting, James, *Adolf Hitler*. Folkestone: Bailey & Swinfen, 1973.

Cross, Colin, *Adolf Hitler*. London: Hodder & Stoughton, 1973.

Daim, W., *Der Mann, der Hitler Ideen Gab*. Munich: Isar Verlag, 1958.

Davidson, Eugene, *The Making of Adolf Hitler*. London: Macdonald & Jane's, 1978.

Dollmann, Eugene, *Call Me a Coward*. London: William Kimber, 1956.

Duffler, Jost, *Hitler's Städte*. 1978.

Dulles, Allen, *The Secret Surrender*. London: Weidenfeld & Nicolson, 1967.

Estreicher, Karol, *Cultural Losses of Poland*. Cracow, 1945.

Fest, Joachim, *Hitler*. London: Weidenfeld & Nicolson, 1974.

——, *Hitler eine Karriere*. Frankfurt: Ullstein Verlag, 1977.

Frischauer, Willy, *The Rise and Fall of Goering*. London: Four Square Books, 1960.

Fromm, Erich, *The Anatomy of Human Destructiveness*. London: Jonathan Cape, 1973.

Giesler, Hermann, *Ein Anderer Hitler*. Leoni am Starnberger See, Bavaria: Drüffel Verlag, 1978.

Godley, John R., *Van Meegeren: A Case History*. London: Nelson, 1967.

Gollert, Friedrich, *Zwei Jahre Aufbauarbeit*. Warsaw, 1941.

Günther, Hans, *Mein Eindruck von Hitler*. Munich, 1969.

Gruber, Karl, *Ein Politisches Leben*. Vienna: Holden Verlag, 1976.

Grunberger, Richard, *A Social History of the Third Reich*. London: Weidenfeld & Nicolson, 1977.

Hamsher, William, *Albert Speer*. London: Leslie Frewin, 1970.

Hanfstaengel, Eberhard, *Adolf Hitler: The Missing Years*. London: Eyre & Spottiswoode, 1957.

——, *Meisterwerke*. Hanover: Knorr & Hirth, 1965.

Hansen, Walter, *Neue Zielsetzungen*. Hamburg: Hansische Hochschul Zeitung, 1936.

Heiden, C., *Adolf Hitler*. London: Pordes, 1967.

Hermes, Richard, *Witz contra Nazi*. Hamburg: Morave & Scheffelt Verlag, 1946.

Heuss, Theodor, *Hitler's Weg*. Stuttgart: Union Verlag, 1932.

Hinz, Berthold, *Malerei im deutschen Faschismus*. Amsterdam: Arbeiderspens, 1974.

——, *Art in the Third Reich*. Oxford: Blackwell, 1980.

H.M. Stationery Office, *The Nazi Culture in Poland*. London, 1945.

Hitler, Adolf, *Mein Kampf*. London: Secker & Warburg, 1969.

Hitler, Bridget, *The Memoirs of Bridget Hitler*. London: Duckworth, 1979.

Hoettl, Wilhelm, *The Secret Front*. London: Weidenfeld & Nicolson, 1953.

Hoffmann, Heinrich, *Hitler Was My Friend*. London: Burke, 1955.

Hoffmann, Peter, *Hitler's Personal Security*. London: Macmillan, 1979.

Howe, Thomas, *Saltmines and Castles*. Indianapolis, Ind.: Bobbs-Merrill, 1946.

Institut für Zeitgeschichte, *Widerstand und Verfolgung in Bayern 1933–45 Vierteljahrhefte*. Munich, 1975.

Jedlicka, Ludwig, *Vom Alten zum Neuen Österreich*. St Pölten, 1975.

Jetzinger, Franz, *Hitler's Youth*. London: Hutchinson, 1958.

Kemkpa, Erich, *Ich Habe Hitler Verbrannt*. Munich: Kyrburg Verlag, 1951.

Kempowski, Walter, *Haben sie Hitler gesehen*. Munich, 1973.

Koehler, Gerhard, *Kunstanschauung*. Munich, 1937.

Kubizek, August, *Young Hitler*. London: W.H. Allen, 1954.

——, *Adolf Hitler, mein Jugendfreund*. Graz: Leopold Stocker Verlag, 1966.

Langer, Walter C., *The Mind of Adolf Hitler*. London: Secker & Warburg, 1973.

Lehman Haupt, Hellmut, *Art under Dictatorship*. New York: Oxford University Press, 1954.

Ludecke, Curt, *I Knew Hitler*. New York: E. Scribner, 1937.

Luza, Radonai, *Österreich und die Grossdeutsche Idee*. Vienna: Bohlaus Nachfolg, 1977.

Mahan, J. A., *Vienna Yesterday and Today*. New York: Brentano, 1928.

Martin, Kurt, *Der Maler Emanuel Fohn*. Munich, 1965.

Maser, Werner, *Legende, Mythos, Wirklichkeit*. Esslingen: Bechtle Verlag, 1972.

——, *Frühgeschichte der NSDAP*. Stuttgart, 1973.

——, *Adolf Hitler: Mein Kampf*. Esslingen: Bechtle Verlag, 1974.

——, *Nüremberg*. London: Allen Lane, 1979.

Maser, Werner, *Hitlers Briefe und Notizen*. Düsseldorf: Econ Verlag, 1973.

Mayer Lowewenschwert, E., *Schönerer*. Vienna, 1938.

Mihan, George, *Looted Treasure*. London: Alliance Press, 1944.

Ministry of Culture & Art, Warsaw, *Warsaw Accuses*. 1945.

Minott, Rodney, *The Fortress That Never Was*. London: Longman, 1954.

Moiseiwitsch, Maurice, *The Van Meegeren Mystery*. London: Arthur Barker, 1964.

Mosley, Leonard, *The Reichsmarshall*. London: Weidenfeld & Nicolson, 1974.

Mullaly, Frederic, *Hitler Has Won*. London: Macmillan, 1975.

Neumann, Robert, *Pictorial History of the Third Reich*. New York: Bantam Books, 1967.

Oechsener, Frederick, *This Is the Enemy*. London: Heinemann, 1943.

Payne, Robert, *Life and Death of Adolf Hitler*. London: Jonathan Cape, 1973.

Picker, Henry, *Hitlers Tischgespräche*. Stuttgart: Seewald Verlag, 1977.

Poechmueller, ———?, *Weltkunstschätze in Gefahr*. Salzburg, 1948.

Rabitsch, Hugo, *Aus Hitlers Jugendzeit*. Munich: Dr Volks Verlag, 1938.

Rogner, P. Klaus (Ed.), *Verlorene Werke der Malerei*. Munich: Friedrich Adolf Ackermanns Kunstverlag, 1965.

Roh, Franz, *Entartete Kunst*. Hanover: Fackelträger Verlag, 1962.

Rorimer, James Joseph, and Rabin, Gilbert, *Survival*. New York: Abelard Press, 1950.

Rosenberg, Alfred, *Revolution in der Bildenden Kunst?* Munich: Eher Verlag, 1934.

Roxan, David, and Wanstall, Ken, *The Jackdaws of Linz*. London: Cassell, 1964.

Rudolf, E. V. von, *Schönerer*. Munich, 1938.

Schact, Horace Hjalmar, *My First Seventy-Six Years*. London: Allan Wingate, 1955.

Schellenberg, Walter, *Schellenberg Memoirs*. London: André Deutsch, 1956.

Schmidt, Paul, *Hitler's Interpreter*. London: Heinemann, 1951.

Schnee, Heinrich, *Karl Lueger*. Berlin: Dunker & Humblot, 1960.

Seydewitz, Max, *Zerstörung und Wiederaufbau von Dresden*. Berlin: Kongress verlag, 1955.

Slapnicka, Harry, *Oberösterreich als es Oberdonau hiess*. Linz: Oberösterreichischer Landes Verlag, 1978.

Smith, Bradley F., *Hitler: His Family, Childhood and Youth.* Stanford, Calif.: Hoover Institution, 1967.

Speer, Albert, *Inside the Third Reich.* London: Weidenfeld & Nicolson, 1970.

——, *Spandauer Tagebücher.* Berlin: Ullstein Verlag, 1975.

Taylor, Alan J. P., *The Habsburg Monarchy 1809–1918.* Harmondsworth, Middx: Penguin, 1976.

Toland, John, *Hitler.* London: Doubleday, 1978.

Valland, Rose, *Le Front de L'Art.* Paris: Librairie Plon, 1961.

Waite, Robert G. L., *The Psychopathic God: Adolf Hitler.* New York: Basic Books, 1977.

ACKNOWLEDGEMENTS

The author is grateful for the co-operation of museum authorities and government departments in Austria, the Federal Republic of Germany, Italy and Poland. He would also like to thank the following people who provided him with additional information:

In Austria: Dr Felix Czeike, City of Vienna Archives; Dr Walter Czerny, Vienna Academy of Fine Arts; Dr Wilhelm Hoettl, Dr Hermann Horky, Linz Tourist Office; Herr W. Kraus, Vienna Tourist Board; Dr Georg Kugler, Kunsthistorisches Museum, Vienna; Dr Fritz Mayerhofer, Director of Linz City Archives; Mrs T. Nickl of Vienna; Dip. Ing. Werner Sarlay of Linz; Dr Wilhelm Schlag, Ministry of Education and Art; Professor Dr Harry Slapnicka, Upper Austrian Archives, Linz; Dr Ulrich Weinzierl, Documentation Centre of the Austrian Resistance, Vienna; and Dr Simon Wiesenthal, Jewish Documentation Centre.

In Germany: Frau Elga Böhm, Wallraf Richarts Museum, Cologne; Professor Hermann Giesler; Professor Knopp, Stiftung Preussischer Kulturbesitz, Berlin; and Frau Dr R. Wankmüller of Munich.

In Great Britain: The Marquess of Bath; Mr Norbert Burda, Austrian National Tourist Office; Dr Wolfgang Fischer of Fischer Fine Art Ltd; Mrs Alby James; Mrs Marietta Powell-Shedden; Mrs Inez Randall; Herr P. Schoenwaldt, Federal German Embassy; and Mr Wynford Vaughan-Thomas.

In Poland: Dr Andrezj Rottermund, National Museum, Warsaw.

In Switzerland: Dr Gottfried von Meiss of Zürich.

In Italy: Dr Rudolfo Siviero, Rome.

The author is indebted, too, to the staff of the following for assisting him in his research: in London the Austrian Institute; the British Library; the Goethe Institute; the Imperial War Museum; the Italian Institute; the Wiener Library; the Polish Central Circulating Library; and also to the Public Record Office, Kew, and the Richmond-upon-Thames Reference Library.

The author and publishers wish to thank the copyright holders concerned for permission to refer to material published in:

Young Hitler by August Kubizek. W. H. Allen (1954).

The Fortress That Never Was by Rodney Minott. Longman (1954).

The Mind of Adolf Hitler by Walter Langer. Secker & Warburg (1973).

Hitler's Youth by Franz Jetzinger. Hutchinson (1969).

Mein Kampf by Adolf Hitler. Secker & Warburg (1969).

The Anatomy of Human Destructiveness by Erich Fromm. Jonathan Cape (1973).

The Making of Adolf Hitler by Eugen Davidson. Macdonald & Jane's (1974).

The Reichsmarshall by Leonard Mosley. Weidenfeld & Nicolson (1974).

Hitler by Joachim Fest. Weidenfeld & Nicolson (1974).

Inside the Third Reich by Albert Speer. Weidenfeld & Nicolson (1970).

The Secret Surrender by Allen Dulles. Weidenfeld & Nicolson (1967).

Art in the Third Reich by Berthold Hinz. Basil Blackwell Publishers (1980).

Art Under Dictatorship by Lehman Haupt. Oxford University Press, New York (1954).

The Psychopathic God: Adolf Hitler by Robert G. L. Waite. Basic Books Inc, New York (1977).

The Jackdaws of Linz by David Roxan and Ken Wanstall. Cassell (1964).

Warsaw Accuses issued by Ministry of Culture & Art, Warsaw (1945).

Le Front de L'Art by Rose Valland. Librarie Plon, Paris (1961).

Legende, Mythos, Wirklichkeit by Prof. Werner Maser. Bechtle Verlag, Munich (1972).

Spandauer Tagebücher by Albert Speer. Ullstein Verlag, Berlin (1975).

Ein Anderer Hitler by Hermann Giesler. Drüffel Verlag, Leoni, Bavaria (1978).

Kunstpolitik des National Sozialismus by Hildegard Brenner. Rowohlt Taschenbuch Verlag, Hamburg (1963).

Entartete Kunst published by Haus der Kunst, Munich (1962).

Jahrbuch Preussischer Kulturbesitz. Grote, Berlin (1962 & 1970).

Verlorene Werke der Malerei. Friederich Adolf Ackermann Kunstverlag, Munich (1965).

Oberösterreich als es Oberdonau Hiess by Harry Slapnicka. Linz (1978).

PICTURE CREDITS

INDEX